INSTRUCTOR'S MANUAL

to accompany

Behrens and Rosen

A Sequence for Academic Writing
Fourth Edition

Lila M. Harper
Central Washington University

Longman

New York Boston San Francisco
London Toronto Sydney Tokyo Singapore Madrid
Mexico City Munich Paris Cape Town Hong Kong Montreal

Instructor's Manual to accompany Behrens and Rosen, *A Sequence for Academic Writing, Fourth Edition*

1 2 3 4 5 6 7 8 9 10–OPM–12 11 10 09

Longman is an
imprint of

www.pearsonhighered.com

ISBN 10: 0-205-67440-2
ISBN 13: 978-0-205-67440-4

CONTENTS

Meeting WPA Outcomes

The Council of Writing Program Administrators' (WPA) statement on first-year composition programs outlines recommended goals for composition programs. While it is recognized that writing is a complex process that requires time and continued practice, the WPA does list outcomes for the first composition classes. (The full statement can be found at http://www.wpacouncil.org/positions/outcomes.html. A version can also be found in *WPA: Writing Program Administration* 23.1/2 (1999): 59-66.)

A Sequence for Academic Writing's approach provides students with ample practice in those areas that the WPA has identified as important outcomes: rhetorical knowledge; critical thinking, reading and writing; writing as a process; and knowledge of conventions. The writing assignment sequence of summary, critique and synthesis re-enforces the understanding of writing as a series of tasks. Each assignment allows students the opportunity to find, evaluate, analyze and synthesize primary and secondary sources. Students learn to "integrate their own ideas with those of others" and are encouraged to see the relationship "among language, knowledge, and power."

CHAPTER 1

Summary, Paraphrase, and Quotation

Academic writing requires many skills, but the basic skills involve the ability to summarize, paraphrase, and quote from source material. This chapter begins with the basics of summary with by focusing on the essay "Will Your Job Be Exported?" by Alan S. Blinder. This essay addresses the recent "off-sourcing" of American service jobs, a theme that is continued in chapter 8 of *A Sequence of Academic Writing*. Students are taken step-by-step through Blinder's argument and shown how to break an argument down into stages of thought, even when there are no thematic headings. Strategies are presented for handling shorter and longer summaries, personal narratives, and information presented in the form of graphs and tables, using the topic of oil consumption as an example. As the students move from one form of information presentation to another, they begin to develop more active ways of interacting with information. These assignments both provide practice in summarizing and demonstrate a student's understanding of a piece of writing. This chapter then continues in its coverage of paraphrase and quotation—skills vital for the rigorous research writing of later chapters.

This chapter can be used to introduce students to the type of reading and writing required in the course by gradually increasing the difficulty of the pieces they are to summarize. The first assignment may use a shorter and less challenging article from an online

1

periodical, the next a longer and more demanding one but still a work intended for a general audience. The final summary may work with an academic article intended for a professional audience. Throughout this process, critical reading techniques and an awareness of audience can be discussed in addition to summarizing.

CHAPTER SUMMARY

Writing Summaries

The summary is a brief restatement of the content of a passage (a group of paragraphs, a chapter, an article, or a book). This restatement should focus on the *central idea* of the passage. A summary may be as brief as one or two sentences (the central idea only) or one paragraph (the central idea and its supporting points), or as lengthy as several paragraphs (the central idea, its supporting points, and some important examples), depending on its purpose. In addition, it will not contain any of the student's opinions. A good summary should be brief, complete, and objective.

One of the challenges of writing a summary is that initially students may not be very familiar with the topic and have little background in the subject. On the other hand, they may have some background, but then have problems maintaining objectivity if they do not agree with the author. Students should strive to understand the issues when reading and be as objective as possible when summarizing. Although restating a central idea and the main points might sound like a simple task, students need to be encouraged to read the editors' footnotes and ask questions if they do not understand the readings. They also should be aware if there is something in their backgrounds that biases their writing of a summary of an article. In the case of Alan Blinder's "Will Your Job Be Exported?" students are immediately presented with an allusion to a figure from the history of Economics. They should not skip over allusions that they are not familiar with, but be willing to use reference sources and dictionaries to better understand their readings.

How to Read Critically

- o   Examine the context.
- o   Identify the audience.
- o   Note the title and subtitle.
- o   Identify the main point.
- o   Identify the subordinate points.
- o   Break the reading into sections.
- o   Distinguish between points, examples, and counterarguments.
- o   Watch for transitions within and between paragraphs.

2

- Look up allusions and vocabulary that may be unfamiliar.
- Read actively and recursively.

How to Write Summaries

- Read the passage carefully.
- Reread.
- Write one-sentence summaries of each stage of thought.
- Write a one- or two-sentence summary of the entire passage.
- Write the first draft of your summary.
- Check your summary against the original passage.
- Revise your summary.

Summarizing Narratives and the Personal Essay

The purpose of a narrative or a personal essay is to tell a story. A student should not write a narrative to summarize a narrative. To summarize either a personal essay or a narrative, a student should give a synopsis or overview of the story's events and relate how these events affect the story's central character. It will likely be a paragraph, at most. Reread the material and make notes in the margin every time the narrative moves from one time to another. When writing the summary, re-create for the audience that sense of a change in time. Notice in the example summary that while the narrative or personal essay is written in the first person, the summary is written in the third person.

Summarizing Figures and Tables

Figures and tables are themselves summaries of complicated data and concepts. The examples presented in Chapter One of *A Sequence of Academic Writing* use different types of figures, tables, and graphs to show oil consumption and world oil reserves. By working with this material, students can see how the visual display of numerical data can highlight different aspects of a research topic.

- Pie Charts show relative proportions or percentages.
- Line and Bar Graphs relate one variable to another. They are effective in showing trends over a period of time or cause-and-effect relationships.
- Tables present numerical data in rows and columns for quick reference and are most effective when the writer wants to emphasize numbers, particularly when a great deal of data is being displayed.

3

Writing Paraphrases

A paraphrase restates the entire sentence, paragraph, etc. in a writer's own words. It is approximately the same length (or even longer) than the original. Paraphrasing is used to make material written in dense, abstract, archaic, or confusing language more presentable.

How to Write Paraphrases

- Make sure that you understand the passage.
- Substitute your own words for those of the passage. Use synonyms where necessary.
- Rearrange your own sentences so that they read smoothly.
- Reorder and restructure your sentences to improve coherence and style.

Using Quotations

A quotation records an author's exact wording. Quotations should be used sparingly. Papers should be made up mostly of summaries and paraphrases of the information a student finds while researching, using quotations for effect. Another author's words may lend credibility to an argument or express something that cannot be adequately paraphrased, but the use of too many quotes weakens an argument by obscuring the student's voice, suggesting a lack of confidence in the argument.

When to Quote

- Use quotations when another writer's language is particularly memorable and will add interest and liveliness to your paper.
- Use quotations when another writer's language is so clear and economical that to make the same point in your own words would be, by comparison, ineffective.
- Use quotation when you want the solid reputation of a source to lend authority and credibility to your own writing.

WRITING/CRITICAL THINKING ACTIVITIES

Note: Internet sources are generally transitory, so if a link given for an activity is no longer available, do a search for the source to see if it is elsewhere or find another suitable source for the activity.

4

Activity One

1. Why is the skill of summarizing important to master?

2. Discuss how summary is used in both academic writing and writing for the workplace. What special projects or assignments might require a summary as either part of the project or assignment or all of it?

3. Why is it difficult for a summary to be truly objective?

4. What does it mean to read actively?

5. What is the difference between a paraphrase and a summary?

6. Why might you paraphrase rather than summarize and vice versa?

7. Discuss two ways to avoid freestanding quotations.

Activity Two
Read "Will Your Job Be Exported?" by Alan S. Blinder (in Chapter One of *A Sequence for Academic Writing*) and respond to the following:

1. Summarize the process of "offshoring" that happens when jobs are moved overseas.

2. Visit the Web site of *The American Prospect* at <http://www.prospect.org>. Based on what you see there, describe the magazine's audience.

3. What is Blinder's attitude toward a college education? Does it have a place in the new economy?

4. List the three main points that Blinder makes about preparing the American workforce for a changing global economy.

Activity Three

1. Go to The Annie E. Casey Foundation Web site at <http://www.kidscount.org/datacenter/compare_results.jsp?i=12>. Write a short paragraph summary for the figure "Births to Females Less than 20 Years of Age."

2. Go to International Shark Attack File: Stats, Trends, Analysis at
   <http://www.flmnh.ufl.edu/fish/sharks/isaf/graphs.htm>.
   Write a short paragraph summary for one of the graphs on shark attack rates.

3. Go to the CNN.com Web site at
   <http://cnn.co.hu/2008/TECH/06/20/solar.house>.
   Write a short paragraph summary of "Solar Panels, Clothesline Help Family Slash Energy Bills."

4. Go to *The Independent* (London) Web site at
    <http://www.independent.co.uk/life-style/health-and-wellbeing/health-news/life-near-a-city-park-can-be-as-healthy-as-out-in-the-country-998212.html>.
   Write a one-sentence summary of "Life Near a City Park Can Be as Healthy as Out in the Country" by Steve Connor (*The Independent* 7 November 2008).

Activity Four

Go to the New York Times Web site at
<http://www.nytimes.com/2008/08/03/science/earth/03jellyfish.html> and read "Stinging Tentacles Offer Hint of Oceans' Decline" by Elisabeth Rosenthal (*New York Times* 3 August 2008) then answer the following questions:

1. What is concerning about the increase in the populations of jellyfish?

2. Where is the increase in population most apparent?

3. What do researchers think might be causing the explosion of jellyfish populations?

4. Are all jellyfish dangerous?

5. Write a paragraph summary of "Stinging Tentacles Offer Hint of Oceans' Decline."

REVISION ACTIVITIES

Activity One

Read Ricardo Bayon's "The Fuel Subsidy We Need" in Chapter Three of *A Sequence for Academic Writing,* and then study the four sample summaries below. Decide which the best summary is for "The Fuel Subsidy We Need" and defend your answer in a short paragraph. In your response, consider the following: Is the source of the summary

6

explicitly identified? Is the sample summary sufficiently objective? Is the summary correctly paraphrased, i.e., not overly dependent on the source's language? Does the summary clearly state the thesis? Is the summary accurate? Are transitions used effectively?

Summary #1

Americans have the most energy-dependent economy in the world, consuming 25 percent of the oil produced in the world. America is too dependent on Saudi Arabia for its oil, so we should develop hydrogen fuel cells. Since the U. S. is dependent on foreign oil, our economy is vulnerable to the effects of turmoil in the Middle East.

Summary #2

In his article "The Fuel Subsidy We Need," Ricardo Bayon argues that the United States should focus on developing hydrogen fuel cells, instead of solar or wind farms, since fuel cells can power cars while not polluting the atmosphere. Fuel cells are used in other countries and shipment has begun to the U. S.

Summary #3

In his article "The Fuel Subsidy We Need," Ricardo Bayon explains that the U. S. economy is too dependent on foreign oil. Rather than allowing Middle Eastern oil-producing countries to control the price of oil, and thus our economy, we should make greater use of alternative energy sources such as solar power, windmills, and hydrogen fuel cells. Since hydrogen fuel cells can power cars without pollution, are quiet, and are already in use, hydrogen fuel technology is the best choice for making Americans less oil dependent.

Summary #4

Ricardo Bayon is concerned with the American economy's dependence on oil production. He points out that even if we purchase our oil from non-Middle Eastern countries, we are still entangled in Middle East politics since the Persian Gulf countries control the oil pricing. In this article, he argues that hydrogen fuel technology is the best choice for an alternative energy source that will lessen our industry's need for oil.

STUDENT WEB RESOURCES

University of Victoria English Department. The UVic Writer's Guide: Summaries
http://Web.uvic.ca/wguide/Pages/summariesTOC.html
> This site provides instructions on writing summaries and includes example summaries.

Purdue University. Purdue Online Writing Lab: Quoting, Paraphrasing, and Summarizing
http://owl.english.purdue.edu/owl/resource/563/01/
> This site discusses quotations, paraphrases, and summaries, including definitions of the terms. A practice exercise is included as well.

C. Sandra Jamieson. Drew University. Resources for Writers: Summary Writing
http://www.users.drew.edu/~sjamieso/Summary.html
> This site explains the importance of summarizing as a necessary component of most other kinds of writing and its importance in note taking, too.

How to Write a Summary. San Diego State University
http://www.wou.edu/provost/library/instruct/writing%20a%20summary-1.pdf
> This site provides an example of how to summarize legal principles by annotating a passage titled "Global Implications of Patent Law Variation."

Bangkok Post Educational Services. Introduction: Short and to the Point
http://www.bangkokpost.net/education/latest/tija1899.htm
> This site is designed primarily for those whose first language is not English. It covers the basics of summarizing and provides exercises, as well.

Columbia University. School of Social Work. Writing Center Handouts.
http://www.columbia.edu/cu/ssw/write/handouts/summary.html
> This site breaks the summarizing process down into steps.

Colorado State University. Writing Guides. Writing Summaries.
http://writing.colostate.edu/guides/documents/standsum/
> This site provides guidelines for incorporating source material into the summary.

Saint Cloud State University. LEO: Literacy Education Online. Using Quotations.
http://leo.stcloudstate.edu/research/usingquotes.html
> This site provides guidelines for using quotations and incorporating quoted material in essays.

8

Purdue University Online Writing Lab. Quotation Marks.
http://owl.english.purdue.edu/handouts/grammar/g_quote.html
This site provides guidelines for using quotations and has a link to an exercise on using quotation marks.

Times Topics. Abraham Lincoln.
http://topics.nytimes.com/top/reference/timestopics/people/l/abraham_lincoln/index.html?inline=nyt-per
The *New York Times* provides a Web site with a list of resources on Abraham Lincoln that can supplement the selection "The Political Genius of Abraham Lincoln" by Doris Kearns Goodwin in chapter 1.

CHAPTER 2

Critical Reading and Critique

An important skill required in academic writing is critical reading. For many students, this may be the most difficult skill to master. Many college students are used to reading passively and do not regularly engage with a writer's argument. Because a good argument paper may require substantial background reading, it is important to check on the students' background and try to motivate the class involvement by connecting the reading with the students' own experiences. Damon Beres' essay "The Common App Fallacy" in this chapter provides an opportunity to discuss with the class their own experiences with college application forms. Although students may grapple with critical reading because it takes more effort than the reading they are accustomed to, instructors should point out the potential of academic reading to increase one's knowledge.

In teaching critical reading, the instructor may find it helpful to discuss other kinds of texts that students are familiar with, such as Web sites and advertisements, as a way to introduce what it means to critique something. Students can then read at least one or two of the same articles assigned in Chapter 1 for summarizing, but this time the articles are revisited using the critique techniques outlined in this chapter. At least one article from the text is critiqued as a major assignment. Assign the article to the students, since having students choose their own articles for this first major critique is too cumbersome for both students and the instructor.

CHAPTER SUMMARY

Reading Critically

Reading critically involves both summarizing and evaluating a piece of writing. For academic writing, you seek information on a topic. Sources for a topic are not equally valuable, however, so you must learn to discern what is and isn't useful to you. To determine validity in your source material, ask yourself the following questions about the passages, articles, and books that you read:

- o   What is the author's purpose in writing?
- o   Does he or she succeed in this purpose?
- o   To what extent do you agree with the author?

11

What Is the Author's Purpose?

o Identify the author's thesis.
o Identify the author's purpose: to inform, to persuade, or to entertain?
o Determine how successful the author has been.

Does He or She Succeed in This Purpose?

Informative Writing. If the author's purpose is to inform, first consider answers to any who, what, where, when, and how questions related to the subject matter of the article. Next, consider its accuracy, significance, and fair interpretation.

Persuasive Writing. If the author's purpose is to persuade, assess its validity by determining whether the author has accomplished the following:

o Clearly defined key terms
o Used information fairly
o Argued logically and not fallaciously

Logical Fallacies

o Emotionally Loaded Terms—using terms with powerful connotations to sway the reader's emotions
o Ad Hominem Argument—rejecting the opposing views by attacking the person who holds them
o Faulty Cause and Effect—assuming one event caused another without proving it
o Either/Or Reasoning—assuming only two possibilities for a given situation exist
o Hasty Generalization—drawing conclusions from too little evidence or unrepresentative evidence
o False Analogy—assuming two things that are similar in one way are also similar in other ways
o Begging the Question—assuming as a proven fact the very thesis being argued
o Non Sequitur—concluding with a point that does not logically follow from a premise
o Oversimplification—offering easy solutions for complicated problems

12

To What Extent Do You Agree With the Author?

Distinguish between the argument's merits and your agreement or disagreement with the author's views. You may agree with an author's views, but you might find that the work contains flaws in logic or inaccuracies in statements of fact. On the other hand, you might find that although you disagree with the author's point of view, you find that the work is logically sound and reasonable. The best approach to your critique, then, is twofold. First, you will identify the author's purpose and design; second, you will respond with points of agreement and disagreement as you evaluate the validity of the argument. As you respond to the work, you should state your position clearly and provide evidence for your position.

WRITING/CRITICAL THINKING ACTIVITIES

Note: Internet sources are generally transitory, so if a link given for an activity is no longer available, do a search for the source using a search engine to see if it is elsewhere or find another suitable source for the activity.

Activity One

Read "Broken Ranks," by Amy Graham and Nicholas Thompson, which may be accessed at
<http://www.washingtonmonthly.com/features/2001/0109.graham.thompson.html>.

Use complete sentences to respond to the following:

1. Who are the authors, and what is the title of the article? What is the article's main argument?

2. Summarize the article's main points. Discuss the authors' purpose in writing the article.

3. Assess the validity of the article. Follow the links on the authors' names to read about their backgrounds. Do their backgrounds affect the validity of their argument in any way?

4. Respond to the authors' views. Do you agree or disagree with their views? Discuss your reasons.

5. State your conclusions about the validity of the piece. Were the authors successful in achieving their purpose? Did they omit important information? Did they make claims that they did not support with evidence?

6. Using your answers to the questions above, write a critique of this article.

Activity Two

Read "President Bush Discusses Climate Change," a speech given in April 16, 2008. A transcript may be accessed at <http://www.whitehouse.gov/news/releases/2008/04/20080416-6.html>.

Use complete sentences to respond to the following:

1. What is President Bush's main argument?

2. Summarize the speech's main points.

3. Respond to the president's views. Do you agree or disagree with his views? Discuss your reasons.

4. State your conclusions about the validity of the speech. Was the president successful in achieving his purpose? Did he omit important information? Did he make claims that he did not support with evidence?

5. Using your answers to the questions above, write a critique of the president's climate change speech.

Activity Three

Use complete sentences to respond to the following:

1. Can you disagree with an author's view and still evaluate the presentation of his argument fairly? Why or why not?

2. Read "Regulating Video Games: Must Government Mind Our Children?" by Adam Thierer, which may be accessed on the Cato Institute Web site at <http://www.cato.org/tech/tk/030624-tk.html>. Write a short critique of this article.

14

Activity Four

Read Damon Beres' "The Common APP Fallacy" in Chapter 2 of *A Sequence for Academic Writing*. As you read, sort out the background and context for this article. If you filled out a college application form like the APP, Beres' feelings may resonate with you; if you are not familiar with these forms, you may want to do a little research by visiting the Common Application Web site at <www.commonapp.org> and review their common questions section.

In your journal (or on paper or in a Word file), first note the points Beres makes about the Common Application form. Look for assumptions he makes about how the college application experience should proceed and evaluate them. To what degree do you agree with Beres? Are there any factual discrepancies? For example, the Common Application Web site says they are nonprofit, yet Beres believes it is a profitable operation. Then consider Beres' attitude toward other students. How does he characterize high school students? Pay attention to emotionally loaded language and the use of metaphors. Try to locate the source of Beres' frustration.

Now organize your response. On another page, identify Beres' thesis and supporting points. Respond to them. To what extent do you agree and to what extent do you disagree? Explain why you responded the way you did.

REVISION ACTIVITIES

Activity One

Read the position statements written in response to the question of whether schools should ban water bottles on the *American Teacher* Web page (February 2008), which may be accessed at
< http://www.aft.org/pubs-reports/american_teacher/feb08/speakout_yes.htm>.
Lucille Hollander writes, "Yes, There are Better Alternatives," and Jane Bluestein writes, "No, It's a Healthy Accommodation." Choose one position to respond to. Are any logical fallacies evident in this argument? What kind(s)? Provide examples.

15

Activity Two

Read the wire story, "Ban Likely to Cut Black Enrollment" (Aug. 12, 2001), which may be accessed at <http://speakout.com/activism/apstories/10073-1.html>. Are any logical fallacies evident in this article? What kind(s)? Provide examples.

STUDENT WEB RESOURCES

Academic Writing: Critical Reviews
<http://www.wisc.edu/writing/Handbook/CriNonfiction.html>
> The Writing Center at the University of Wisconsin-Madison provides many helpful links for various writing assignments, one of which is a critique.

Writing Book Reviews
<http://www.indiana.edu/~wts/pamphlets/book_reviews.shtml>
> The Writing Tutorial Services Center at Indiana University Bloomington provides a good discussion of critiquing a book, which can be applied to an article critique.

The Nizkor Project
<http://www.nizkor.org/features/fallacies/>
> Dr. Michael C. Labossiere provides examples of 42 informal logical fallacies. (Only a few examples are discussed in *A Sequence for Academic Writing*.)

The Fallacy Files
<http://www.fallacyfiles.org>
> The Fallacy Files is a comprehensive site that provides explanations of fallacies with examples from books, newspapers, magazines, newsletters, and fundraising letters.

Persuasive Writing
<www.uvsc.edu/owl/info/pdf/types_of_writing/persuasive.pdf>
> From the Online Writing Lab at Utah Valley State College, this site explains the basics of persuasive writing.

Logical Fallacies: An Encyclopedia of Errors of Reasoning
<http://www.logicalfallacies.info/>
> This is an entire Web site devoted to describing types of logical fallacies.

Brian Yoder's Fallacy Zoo
< http://www.goodart.org/fallazoo.htm>
> A humorous guide to classical fallacies.

16

Bruce Thompson's Fallacy Page

< http://www.cuyamaca.edu/brucethompson/Fallacies/intro_fallacies.asp>

Professor Thompson has provided lots of useful examples and exercises on this site for his students at Cuyamaca College.

17

CHAPTER 3

Explanatory Synthesis

This chapter works well as an introduction to writing a research paper. Up to this point, students have worked with quoting, paraphrasing, summarizing, and critiquing. The next logical step is to have them discuss more than one source in a paper. This chapter helps prepare students to incorporate sources into the discussion of a paper topic. Working on thesis statements that suggest an explanation rather than an argument will also help students understand the difference between explanatory and argument syntheses.

CHAPTER SUMMARY

What is a Synthesis?

A synthesis is a written discussion that draws on two or more sources in support of an original claim. The writer will establish the credibility of sources, infer connections across sources, and summarize, quote, and paraphrase sources judiciously, to further the paper's claim. Students might imagine the synthesis as a symphony, of sorts: source authors are the instruments; the student is, in turns, conductor, instrument (as a source in his or her own right), and composer, calling on others in building the composition.

How to Write Syntheses

Here are a few guidelines to follow that will help you organize and write your paper:

- o Consider your purpose in writing.
- o Select and carefully read your sources.
- o Take notes on your reading.
- o Formulate a thesis.
- o Decide how you will use your source material.
- o Develop an organizational plan.
- o Draft the topic sentences for the main sections.
- o Write the first draft of your synthesis.
- o Document your sources.
- o Revise your synthesis.

19

Remember that all writing is a recursive process, so in writing your synthesis, you may or may not follow these guidelines step by step.

There are two main types of syntheses: the explanatory synthesis (discussed in Chapter 3) and the argument synthesis (discussed in Chapter 4). Whereas an argument synthesis argues a particular point, an explanatory synthesis helps readers understand a topic. To explore a subject, the subject should be divided it into its component parts and presented to the reader in a clear and orderly fashion. The information must be presented objectively, without judgment. Doing so will require a precise thesis statement on which to base information, one that is clearly supported by all the sources.

Students may be tempted to organize their synthesis by source, by linking together a series of source summaries. This approach, however, does not promote a true dialogue between the ideas expressed in the sources. Source organization will also present organization problems as students move toward writing longer papers. When writing in the disciplines, source organization is the mark of a poorly written review of literature discussions.

It is important at this point to stress organizing the synthesis by idea, rather than source. Blending shared ideas among sources will both promote a deeper exploration of the issue and increase students' engagement with their writing.

WRITING/CRITICAL THINKING ACTIVITIES

Note: Internet sources are generally transitory, so if a link given for an activity is no longer available, do a search for the source to see if it is elsewhere or find another suitable source for the activity.

Activity One

Read over a few of the articles on e-mail etiquette listed below. Craft a thesis statement to explain some aspect of e-mail etiquette based on at least three of the articles listed below. Once you have a thesis, compose a short, explanatory synthesis (approximately one paragraph). Document any sources you quote, summarize, or paraphrase by citing them within your paragraph; don't worry about a works cited page.

"Toward an Ethics and Etiquette for Electronic Mail."
<http://www.rand.org/pubs/reports/R3283/index.html>
> The RAND corporation Web site offers a link to the full 1985 report on the use of e-mail. The report offers several examples of poorly written and confusing e-mails.

"E-Mail Etiquette."
<http://www.emailreplies.com>
> This Web site is oriented toward businesses and is designed to educate employees about effective email usage. Company liability issues are discussed.

"The Ten Commandments of E-Mail" by Tom Spring.
<http://www.pcworld.com/article/id,10306-page,1/article.html>
> An article published in *PCWorld* (March 29, 1999)

"12 Tips for Better E-Mail Etiquette."
<http://office.microsoft.com/en-us/outlook/HA012054101033.aspx>
> Laura Stack, president of The Productivity Pro, a business consulting firm, offers guidelines for email usage.

"E-Mail Etiquette."
<http://www.iwillfollow.com/email.htm>
> Essay featured on the *Iwillfollow* Web site.

"Email Etiquette."
<http://careerplanning.about.com/od/communication/a/email_etiquette.htm>
> Guidelines by Dawn Rosenberg McKay featured on the *About.Com* career planning Web site.

"E-Mail Etiquette."
<http://owl.english.purdue.edu/owl/resource/636/01/>
> From the Purdue OWL site, an essay by Stephanie Williams Hughes that was recently updated.

"E mail Etiquette and Common Sense"
<http://ri.essortment.com/emailetiquet_reaq.htm>
> Essay published on *Pagewise Inc.* Web site.

"Lepak's Guide to Style and Electronic Communication"
<http://www.lepak.com/emailet.html>
> Essay featured on the *Lepak.com* Web site.

"Email Etiquette (for the uninformed or intentionally rude)"
<http://ransompark.users2.50megs.com/page12.html>
    Essay by Alan Keith, ranger of Ransom Park, Texas. This is posted on a humorous
    personal Web site.

"Email Netiquette"
<http://www.library.yale.edu/training/netiquette/index.html>
    This site offers training to the staff at Yale University Library on how to properly use
    email. There is a helpful source list at the end.

Activity Two

Read over a few of the articles on the use of over-the-counter medicines on children
listed below. Craft a thesis statement to explain why doctors are calling for changes in the
use of cold remedies for children. Once you have a thesis, compose a short, explanatory
synthesis (approximately one paragraph). Document any sources you quote, summarize,
or paraphrase by citing them within your paragraph; don't worry about a works cited
page for this activity.

"Over-the-Counter Medicine: Kids Aren't Just Small Adults"
<http://eclkc.ohs.acf.hhs.gov/hslc/For%20Parents/Safe%20and%20Healthy%20Family/H
ealth/KidsArentJust.htm>
    A report from the U.S. Department of Health and Human Services.

"FDA Panel: Don't Use Cold Meds in Kids under 6"
< http://www.msnbc.msn.com/id/21376717/>
    An October 19, 2007 report from the Associated Press found on the MSNBC Web
    site.

"Over the Counter but No Longer Under the Radar—Pediatric Cough and Cold
Medications"
< http://content.nejm.org/cgi/content/full/357/23/2321>
    In this editorial from the *New England Journal of Medicine* (December 6, 2007),
    Joshua M. Sharfstein, Marisa North, and Janet R. Serwint give a regulatory history
    of children's cold medicine.

"F.D.A. Panel Urges Ban on Medicine for Child Colds"
< http://www.nytimes.com/2007/10/20/washington/20fda.html>
    This article by Gardiner Harris, published in the *New York Times* (October 20, 2007),
    explains the decision by the Food and Drug Administration to ban over-the-counter
    cold products for children under the age of 6.

22

Activity Three

Read over a few of the articles on video game playing and socialization skills listed below. Craft a thesis statement to explain some aspect of this issue based on at least three of the articles listed below. Carefully notice the date of publication. Once you have a thesis, compose a short, explanatory synthesis (approximately one paragraph). Document any sources you quote, summarize, or paraphrase by citing them within your paragraph; don't worry about a works cited page.

"Online Games Provide Social Connection"
<http://www.cbsnews.com/stories/2006/08/18/health/webmd/main1912860.shtml>
> This article on the CBS News Web Site reports on a study of multiplayer online games and socialization that was published in the July 2006 issue of the *Journal of Computer-Mediated Communication.*

"Socializing: Healthier Choice than Playing Video Games"
<http://media.www.asuherald.com/media/storage/paper898/news/2007/09/24/Opinion/So cializing.Healthier.Choice.Than.Playing.Video.Games-2987762.shtml>
> Editorial by Sam Pierce published in the student newspaper, *The Herald* of Arkansas State University, published Sept. 24, 2007.

"Teens, Video Games and Civics"
<http://www.pewinternet.org/PPF/r/263/report_display.asp>
> This report (September 16, 2008) on a survey conducted by the Pew Internet and American Life Project concludes that there is social interaction in gaming experiences.

"Content-Centered Conversations: The Pew Internet Report on Teens and Social Media"
<http://gumption.typepad.com/blog/2008/01/content-centere.html>
> On his blog, *Gumption*, Joe McCarthy reflects on his reading of the Pew Report and the concept of "object-centered sociality," while also providing several internal links to definitions of terms.

STUDENT WEB RESOURCES

Resources for Writers: Synthesis Writing
<http://www.users.drew.edu/~sjamieso/Synthesis.htm#key%20features>
    C. Sandra Jamieson of Drew University provides a thorough discussion of synthesis writing in daily life to synthesis writing outside of college.

Explanatory Synthesis Checklist
<http://users.drew.edu/sminegar/Explanatory%20Synthesis%20Checklist.htm>
    Also from Drew University, Sarah Minegar provides a short checklist for an explanatory synthesis assignment.

The Role of Hypermedia in Synthesis Writing
<http://computersandcomposition.osu.edu/archives/v10/10_2_html/10_2_6_Palumbo.html>
    David B. Palumbo and Doris Prater discuss the role of hypermedia in synthesis writing in the online journal *Computers and Composition*, volume 9, no. 2 (1993), pages 59-70.

CHAPTER 4

The Argument Synthesis

This chapter presents the argument synthesis, which is more challenging than the explanatory synthesis because students must evaluate the arguments of others and make their own arguments. Because students are often inexperienced in evaluating arguments, a good overview of logical fallacies may be valuable at this point so that as they read the sample articles they will be actively engaged in defining the persuasive techniques used in their readings. The chapter presents several readings on the difficult problem of balancing privacy and safety after the shootings at Virginia Tech. Students are provided with the report of a review panel that was presented to the governor, along with the language of the Family Educational Rights and Privacy Act (FERPA). Using logical argumentation, along with the report and legal background, the class can consider differing positions on the topic, take a position, and support it.

The tragedy at Virginia Tech has motivated all campuses to reexamine how they take precautions and communicate to the campus community in times of danger. The class might begin this topic with a class discussion on what communication procedures are in place on your campus in case of an emergency. If your campus has something similar to a "student alert form" mentioned in "Law Limit Schools Even After Alarms" by Jeff Gammage and Stacey Burling (in this chapter), this can be discussed. Your campus health center may also be contacted for information on how students can receive counseling help and how privacy laws are implemented on campus. Similarly, campus security may be willing to provide information on emergency procedures.

A model student essay is provided in this chapter. As students read through it, they might ask if the assumption that student privacy laws are important is earned. If your campus has had a recent episode of violence, students will feel a need for greater protection and, possibly, a willingness to roll back FERPA privacy rights. Ask if the writer's assumption about the importance of privacy is persuasive if the readers do not initially agree with that assumption.

Students may struggle as they try to balance their own sense of safety on campus with their right to privacy. As they carefully read through the legal discussions on the federal privacy laws, however, students may conclude that the federal privacy laws are not as restrictive as they first appear and that some restrictions are really the result of policies originating on campus.

25

CHAPTER SUMMARY

The Elements of Argument

The argument synthesis discusses a claim about which reasonable people could disagree, and the purpose of it is to persuade a reader to agree with the claim.

- o Claim—a proposition or conclusion to be proved
- o Support—facts or expert opinions
- o Assumption—an underlying belief or principle about some aspect of the world and how it operates
- o Analysis—application of the principles that underlie our assumptions to the specific evidence

The Three Appeals of Argument

When arguing, speakers and writers have never relied on logic alone to persuade an audience. Besides evidence (logos), speakers and writers must prove their credibility (ethos) to the audience, and may even attempt to affect the emotions (pathos) of the audience.

Logos (appeal to reason). Deductive reasoning contains three parts: a generalization, a specific case related to that generalization, and a conclusion—in other words, the claim, the support, and the assumption. Inductive reasoning begins with specific pieces of evidence and draws a conclusion from the evidence. The evidence used in inductive reasoning must be sufficient to support the conclusion. Both types of reasoning should include sufficient facts and other supporting details to back up their claims.

Ethos (appeal to the intellectual or moral authority of the speaker or writer). Ethos refers to how well the writer presents himself or herself. The person making the argument must be credible in order for the reader to consider his or her assumptions and conclusions valid. An audience also considers whether the person making the argument seems knowledgeable and reasonable. Questions an audience might ask include "Are counterarguments presented?" and "Are opponents and their arguments treated with fairness and respect?"

Pathos (appeal to emotion). Pathos refers to the writer's ability to evoke the emotions of his or her readers. A writer may present a story to illustrate an issue: for example, he or she may describe the reactions of the fetus during an abortion procedure. The writer may tap into one or a few emotions, such as sadness, fear, anger, patriotism, love, etc., but must do so effectively without being manipulative.

Developing and Organizing the Support for Your Arguments

Using the three appeals of argument as your guide, categorize your support as being either evidence or motivational appeals. Evidence constitutes logos; motivational appeals constitute ethos and pathos.

- o   Summarize, paraphrase, and quote supporting evidence.
- o   Provide various types of evidence and motivational appeals.
- o   Use climactic order.
- o   Use logical or conventional order:
    - • Problem/solution
    - • Two sides of a controversy
    - • Comparison-contrast
        - • Discipline-specific organizational strategies
- o   Present and respond to counterarguments (arguments against your claim).
- o   Use concession for ethical appeal.
- o   Avoid common fallacies in developing and using support.

The Comparison-Contrast Synthesis

- o   Comparison examines similarities.
- o   Contrast examines differences.

Use criteria to guide a comparison-contrast synthesis. The sources you use will have based their judgments on certain criteria that they make about their topic. Review your sources to identify their criteria for making those judgments and choose significant criteria to analyze in your comparison to highlight subtle and significant differences between your sources.

Organization by Criteria

- o   Introduce the essay; lead to thesis.
- o   Criterion I
    - • Discuss what author A says about this point.
    - • Discuss what author B says about this point, comparing and contrasting B's treatment with A's.

27

- o Criterion II (Continue this procedure throughout the essay until you have completed your comparison.)
  - Discuss what author A says about this point.
  - Discuss what author B says about this point, comparing and contrasting B's treatment with A's.
- o Conclude the essay.

WRITING/CRITICAL THINKING ACTIVITIES

Note: Internet sources are generally transitory, so if a link given for an activity is no longer available, do a search for the source to see if it is elsewhere or find another suitable source for the activity.

Activity One

Read "Bush's Un-American and Immoral Call for 'National Service'" by Alex Epstein <http://www.aynrand.org/site/News2?page=NewsArticle&id=5319>.

1. Are any logical fallacies evident in this article? What kind(s)? Provide examples.

2. Scan Alex Epstein's Web page <http://www.alexepstein.com/> to learn more about Al Norman, the author of "Bush's Un-American and Immoral Call for 'National Service.'" Does his background affect his credibility in any way?

3. Discuss the author's tone and how it affects the effectiveness of the essay.

Activity Two

Read "Privacy Concerns about U. S. Database" on *Inside Higher Ed* at <http://insidehighered.com/news/2008/11/19/org>
and discuss any examples of pathos, logos, and/or ethos evident in the article or in the readers' comments. Be sure to support your answers.

28

Activity Three

Read the Oct. 16, 2008 amendment to the FERPA found at
<http://edocket.access.gpo.gov/2008/E8-24608.htm>,
which grants waivers to the Privacy Act and allows information to be shared. Discuss how this amendment might impact a discussion of how to balance privacy and safety on campus.

REVISION ACTIVITIES

Activity One

Read one of the four student sample syntheses from Dr. Cassie Carter's course The Evolution of American Thought (spring 1998) that was taught at Michigan State University:
<https://www.msu.edu/user/carterca/samples.htm>
Identify which essay you are using and then respond to the following:

1. What is the author's thesis?

2. Discuss its use of sources.

3. Discuss the appeals used.

STUDENT WEB RESOURCES

Elements of Argument
<http://karn.wright.edu/~sg-ysu/argu.html>
"Elements of Argument" from Youngstown State University's OhioLINK resources contains an overview of argument, from writing and supporting a thesis to planning the structure of an argument.

Argumentation/Persuasion: Logic in Argumentative Writing by the Purdue University Online Writing Lab
<http://owl.english.purdue.edu/handouts/general/gl_argpers.html>
According to Purdue's OWL, this "set of handouts will take you through some of the more common terms and concepts used in formal logical reasoning. You can use these terms and concepts to help you both analyze the arguments of others and generate your own arguments when you write."

The Fallacy Files
<http://www.fallacyfiles.org/>
  The Fallacy Files is a comprehensive site that provides explanations of fallacies with examples from the written books, newspapers, magazines, newsletters, and fundraising letters.

Types of Writing: Persuasive Writing
<www.uvsc.edu/owl/info/pdf/types_of_writing/persuasive.pdf>
  From the Online Writing Lab at Utah Valley State College, this site explains the basics of persuasive writing.

The Art of Rhetoric: Learning How to Use the Three Main Rhetorical Styles
<http://www.rpi.edu/dept/llc/webclass/web/project1/group4/>
  This site will help you to better understand logos, ethos, and pathos, as well as show you how to make your writing more persuasive.

Paragraph Development
<http://www.mccd.edu/faculty/pirov/ParDev9.htm>
  Using an essay on Cesar Chavez's use of boycotts as an example, this site analyzes the structure of a paragraph.

Rhetoric, Logos, Pathos, and Ethos
<http://faculty.millikin.edu/~moconner/writing/workshop7b.html>
  This site provides more complex and detailed definitions of logos, pathos, and ethos.

Rhetorical Strategies: Methods of Presentation
<http://www.unc.edu/~hee/web11fall99/rhetoric.htm>
  This site discusses the concepts of ethos, pathos, and logos in detail and provides pointers on how to use them in your papers effectively.

Three Rhetorical Appeals: Ethos, Pathos, Logos
<http://w.web.umkc.edu/williamsgh/dialogues/225.rhetorical.appeals.html>
  George H. Williams, professor of English at University of Missouri-Kansas City, provides definitions of rhetorical appeals and how to put them together.

Balancing Student Privacy, Campus Security, and Public Safety: Issues for Campus Leaders
< http://www.aascu.org/policy/perspectives/index.htm>
  This is a report from the American Association of State Colleges and Universities (AASC) on the problem of promoting student mental health, safety, and privacy with intellectual freedom and openness.

CHAPTER 5

Analysis

Analysis can be a difficult concept for students to grasp because they may have problems seeing the difference between analysis and summary. This chapter guides students in the process of applying an analytical principle or definition to an object in order to study it more closely, to determine what that object might mean, or to understand its importance. A new section in this edition places greater emphasis on personal perspectives, which may come from the writer's background or life experiences, as a guide for analysis. While an analysis based on a more formal approach would focus on the use of a principle or definition and on developing insights through the use of that principle when examining an object, the more informal-based analysis, while still focused on the act of revealing something, requires that the writer clarify and explain those principles through recounting personal experiences.

More informal approaches to analysis require a certain amount of self-analysis. One approach I use when teaching analysis is to ask students to first explain how they feel about a piece of literature, and then to ask, "why do I feel that way?" Defining the whys of an individual's response help motivate the analysis, while it can also validate individual responses. Personal responses, however, still require the careful use of structure and organization. Students should not feel that they can simply react to a subject without explaining why they are approaching a subject in a particular manner.

This chapter can be used along with the analysis assignments in Chapter 8 of *A Sequence for Academic Writing*.

CHAPTER SUMMARY

What is Analysis?

Analysis makes use of an analytic tool, a principle or definition, to break down something into parts to better understand it as a whole, an activity we engage in daily. It is an essential element of academic inquiry. We analyze things, or critically examine them, to identify their key elements, as well as their causes, or (if they constitute an action of some sort) their possible results. In addition, analysis does not simply ask you to break things down and describe them, but to go further and state what the information arrived at through analysis means.

31

How to Write Textual Analyses

Consider your purpose. What idea do you want to advance? Your analytic insights will only come together in your paper if they are logically related to a central idea. Be prepared to answer the "so what" question.

Read the object under analysis. Try to get a feel for the overall meaning, impressions, and feelings that are conveyed during this initial reading, bearing in mind your purpose for analysis.

Create a context for your analysis. Introduce the object, event, or behavior and explain why analysis is important or necessary. What is the problem? What question should be investigated?

Introduce the key definition or principle. Clearly explain the principle of analysis you will be using and its source. Argue that this principle or definition is valid or valuable for the discussion.

Convert the principle or definition into questions. Having identified a useful definition or principle, apply it to the object under analysis by drafting questions that can be related to that object.

Reread. Once you have gotten an initial feel for the work being analyzed, reread carefully. This time make notes in the margin or on paper indicating how elements of your analytic principle or definition apply to the object under observation. Be sure to look up words or concepts that are confusing or with which you are unfamiliar.

Systematically apply elements of the analytic definition or principle. You might pose questions based on your analytic principle or definition to organize the analysis. Discuss what you find, section-by-section, in clearly indicated parts of the essay. While the object is being described in the process, this is not a summary. Rather the meaning of the object's parts or elements is being examined.

State what is significant about this analysis. What can you see now, having written this analysis that was not apparent on first reading? How has your use of your analytic principle or definition provided new insights into the problem you initially raised?

Draft and Revise your analysis. Revisit your initial problem or issue in order to revise and refine your main idea. Have you answered all the questions that you raised? Are your facts accurate? Does your key definition or principle clearly relate to the elements you selected? Have you responded to dissenting points of view? Add transitions to bridge the

32

discussion of the analytic definition or principle to the object under analysis. Look for areas where your insights might need more clarification. Check for areas where you need to cite your sources.

WRITING/CRITICAL THINKING ACTIVITIES

Note: Internet sources are generally transitory, so if a link given for an activity is no longer available, do a search for the source to see if it is elsewhere or find another suitable source for the activity.

Activity One

Examine the definition of a myth hero developed by Lord Raglan in his book *The Hero: A Study in Tradition, Myth and Dreams* (1936), which is listed at <http://department.monm.edu/classics/Courses/Clas230/MythDocuments/HeroPattern/default.htm>.
Another myth hero pattern is given by Joseph Campbell in his book *The Hero with a Thousand Faces.*

Using these narrative elements, ones that are found in all hero myths across cultures, analyze your favorite action or science fiction film. (The *Star Wars* films offer good examples.) Consider whether such film genres might represent a modern form of the traditional myth hero.

Activity Two

Read the article "Individualism and Alienation in Popular Love Songs, 1930-1999" by sociologist Thomas J. Scheff, which can be found at <http://www.soc.ucsb.edu/faculty/scheff/17.html>.

This article applies a theory of social integration to one type of collective representation, popular love songs. Since modern Western societies focus on individuals rather than relationships, we would expect individualist, rather than relational patterns in U. S. popular lyrics. By examining the language of titles in the most popular American songs over a 70-year period, Scheff has classified the lyrics into three main types of discourse: heartbreak, infatuation, and love. He notes, however, that there is an increase in the indications of alienation in romance lyrics. In particular, Scheff examines the theme of "love at first sight."

33

As Scheff ends his analysis with the year 1999, you may ask whether his conclusions also apply to popular love songs after 2000. Making use of the theory of social integration as outlined by Scheff, select five popular post-2000 love songs and analyze their lyrics.

Some questions you might raise are:
> Is alienation increasing in post-2000 romance lyrics?
> Are the three love forms, heartbreak, infatuation and love, still apparent today?
> Are there more crossover, hybrid forms of romance songs?
> Is the theme of the isolated love still apparent in post-2000 lyrics?
> Is there a decrease in the number of lyrics that imply security and solidarity in romantic bonds?
> Do lyrics feature individual desire or mutual love relationships?
> Is music, rather than lyrics, increasingly dominant?
> Are artists making more use of verbal or non-verbal techniques in their musical expression?

Activity Three

Read the essays by Roland Marchand and Dorothy Cohen in Chapter 5 of *A Sequence for Academic Writing*. Using either Marchand or Cohen's analytical principles, analyze an advertisement from Roland Marchand's ad database of American advertisements found at the History Project Web site at the University of California at Davis:
< http://historyproject.ucdavis.edu/resources.php#marchand>.

Describe both the ads' explicit and implicit messages. Be sure to properly cite the advertisement and indicate when it was published.

Activity Four

Read "The Opposite of Sex: Why We're Obsessed with Jane Austen and Regency-Era Romance" by Lianne George on the Web site *Jane Austen Addict*, which can be found at
<http://www.janeaustenaddict.com/theauthor/press/3>.

What principles or definitions is George using in her analysis of why Jane Austen is so popular today? Is she using a cultural outlook to guide her analysis of the popularity of Jane Austen today?

Compare George's analysis with N. Zeynep Yelce's essay, "The Revival of Jane Austen," which can be accessed on the *Cultural Studies Study Group* Web site at
<http://members.tripod.com/~warlight/AUSTEN.html>

34

What principles or definitions is Yelce using? How does this analysis compare to George's?

Now, examine the first paragraph of Sarah Wootton's more formal analysis, "The Byronic in Jane Austen's *Persuasion* and *Pride and Prejudice*," published in the *Modern Language Review* (Jan. 2007), which can be accessed at <http://findarticles.com/p/articles/mi_7026/is_1_102/ai_n28401276/pg_1?tag=artBo dy;col1>.

Explain how these three analyses of Austen's work differ in their analytic approach.

NO REVISION ACTIVITIES FOR CHAPTER FIVE

STUDENT WEB RESOURCES

Abraham Maslow
<http://www.ship.edu/~cgboeree/maslow.html>
> Dr. C. George Boeree, a psychology professor at Shippensburg University, provides biographical information about Abraham Maslow and explains Maslow's Hierarchy of Needs, while also adding some criticism of the theory.

Personality Theories
< http://webspace.ship.edu/cgboer/perscontents.html>
> This Web site is an electronic textbook by Dr. Boeree that he uses to teach undergraduate and graduate courses in Personality Theories.

The following posters are from a class on American Popular Culture: History, Story and Analysis, taught in the fall of 2005 at the Center for New Designs in Learning and Scholarship at Georgetown University.
An Index to all the posters can be found at
<http://cndls.georgetown.edu/applications/postertool/index.cfm?fuseaction=poster.fullLis t&instanceID=23>.

Advertising and the American Dream: Roland Marchand's Apostles of Modernity by Malgorzata Rymsza-Pawlowska
<http://cndls.georgetown.edu/applications/postertool/index.cfm?fuseaction=poster.displa y&posterID=556>
> Malgorzata Rymsza-Pawlowska makes use of Marchand's analytical principles to analyze 1920s-era posters. Additional links are provided to advertising databases.

Roland Marchand: Trends, Visual Clues, and Gender Ideology in Advertising:
Everything You Never Knew You Wanted: 1920-1939 by Marybeth Ihle.
<http://cndls.georgetown.edu/applications/postertool/index.cfm?fuseaction=poster.displa
y&posterID=2129>

 Marybeth Ihle uses Marchland's analytical principles to analyze sanitary napkin
advertisements.

36

CHAPTER 6

Writing as a Process

The first chapters in Part One: Structures provided guidance for the writing of the basic assignments: the summary, the critique, the explanatory synthesis, and the argument synthesis. In Part Two: Strategies, Chapter 6 examines the basic processes used in all academic writing: the interaction between writing and thinking and the research paper. Chapter 6 introduces writing as a thinking process, a model that students can use as they begin to investigate and refine possible topics for research. This chapter can be used as an overview to acquaint students with the kind of work that will be expected of them as they work toward a well-written, well-argued research paper. Experienced writers have internalized writing strategies, methods for developing and structuring a paper; students, however, will need guidance and help in recognizing writing techniques in their readings and encouragement in developing these techniques in their own writing. Additionally, a classroom discussion of the difference between primary and secondary sources will be helpful as students orient themselves to the expectations for scholarly writing. The earlier focus on what makes a good thesis is continued here with a discussion of how to shape a thesis in response to the writer's rhetorical needs.

CHAPTER SUMMARY

The Writing Process

The stages of the writing process presented here stress possible stages or steps that many writers find useful for writing assignments that involve the use of sources. The process is broken down into several stages.

Understanding the Task

The first stage discussed is *understanding the task*. Writing is not confined only to English classes and you should be prepared to write research papers for instructors across a range of academic disciplines. Understanding what is expected of you is the first step. It is important to critically analyze the assignment by focusing on key verbs in the instructions.

Data Gathering

The first stage discussed is *data gathering*. You may use a wide variety of sources as you are assigned different types of papers throughout your college careers, so it is important to know what is expected in a particular assignment. Once the expectations are clear, you will know what type of data (primary or secondary) is appropriate for the assignment.

Invention

The next stage, *invention*, involves the writing that develops as you gather data and narrow the focus of your assignment. There are many terms for this stage of the process: "brainstorming," "outlining," "prewriting," etc. The first three stages of the writing process work together: gathering data provides ideas while invention helps to focus those ideas around some central idea or thesis, which then forces you to gather more data, etc.

Drafting

The fourth stage is the actual *drafting* of a paper. To begin writing a draft, you need to have a working thesis.

Writing a Thesis.

The thesis is a one-sentence summary of a paper's content. It is an assertion that you wish to make about your essay's topic. You will need to work with your thesis until it fits the parameters of the assignment and allows you to accomplish your purpose in writing the essay. Because you might not know exactly what to assert when you first begin your essay, you should start with a working thesis and refine as you go. As you narrow your thesis, you will also narrow your topic. Keep asking yourself the following questions as you proceed:

- Who?
- What aspects?
- Where?
- When?
- How?

38

You might want to begin with a question. During the writing process, you will probably discover the answer to the question that you posed. The answer to your question should be an assertion about your topic. You can narrow and polish your working thesis by writing different assertions for your topic. Thesis statements can be explanatory, mildly argumentative, or strongly argumentative, depending on your purpose for writing and the scope of the task. Eventually, you will narrow your topic and your thesis to something that is manageable.

Introductions

The introduction to an essay orients readers to your topic. It is your first opportunity to interest them and to give them the context needed to understand your assertions. There are many introductory strategies; you will see the most common strategies used over and over again.

- o   Quotation—Use well-phrased remarks to set the context and to "hook" your reader. Be careful not to let the quoted material overshadow your voice. Quote only what you need to make your point clear.
- o   Historical Review—Some readers will be unprepared to follow the issue you discuss without some background information. Give readers enough information to get started, but don't allow your background to be excessive to the point of distraction.
- o   Statement of Thesis—Begin by stating the thesis in the first sentence of your essay.

Conclusions

The conclusion serves as a bridge from the world of your essay back to the world of your reader. Your conclusion should do the following:

- o   Restate the thesis.
- o   Summarize your main points.
- o   Connect your assertion to the world outside the essay.

In discussing the significance of your essay, you can use several strategies:

- o   State the subject's significance.
- o   Call for further research on the topic.
- o   Provide solutions and recommendations.
- o   Relate an anecdote (this is most effective when it is tied to an anecdote in the introduction).

- o   Quote a famous person or an expert on your topic.
- o   Pose a question.
- o   Speculate on what might happen in the future.

Revision

The fifth stage of writing, one that is often overlooked, is revision. Although the word "revision" can be used to describe all the modifications you might make to a paper, two types of revision—large-scale changes and small-scale changes—are covered here. Large-scale revisions deal with the structure of your paper and the content of your paragraphs. Once you have a rough draft of your paper, but before you attempt any revisions, the best thing to do is to set it aside for a couple of days, so that it is somewhat new when you begin your revisions.

One technique you can use for revision is the reverse outline. Begin by printing a draft of your paper and carefully reviewing each of your body paragraphs. In the margins of your paper, note the main point of each body paragraph. If at any time you have difficulty with the main point of a paragraph, you will know that revision is needed in that paragraph. It may be that you have more than one important idea in a paragraph or that you need to make the point more clear. Either way, note your intent for these paragraphs in the margin as well.

Once you have done this with each body paragraph, you can do one of three things. If your rough draft has a working thesis, determine if each point you noted in the margins relates to your working thesis. Or, if you have no thesis up to this point, take each of the points you noted in the margins and craft a thesis based on your points. (It might be helpful to do both, and compare your original thesis statement with the one based on your points.) If you still have trouble finding a thesis, look at the conclusion of your rough draft to see if your ideas are pulled together there. You may also want to look at the points you made to see if any are simply restatements of your thesis.

After you decide on a thesis (whether you keep the one you started with or decide to adopt another), go back and revise the main points of your paragraphs if they need it. Discard any that don't go with your thesis, revise each body paragraph to go with its main point, and then make sure your points are in logical order.

Editing

Once you have revised your paper's large-scale characteristics (thesis, structure, and content), you need to focus on small-scale issues, such as editing sentences for style and correctness. Editing is the sixth stage of writing. When we write rough drafts, we are mainly concerned with getting our ideas down on paper. This often results in there being many simple sentences without many transitions. To make your paper flow better, connect the ideas in your sentences. First, read your paper carefully to see if your sentences are of varying lengths and types. There should be some short sentences and some long sentences, depending on their content. A short sentence adds emphasis when placed after a string of longer ones, while longer sentences provide room for more complex ideas, necessary detail, etc. Then add coordinate and subordinate conjunctions to create compound, complex, and compound-complex sentences from simple sentences. You may also want to add adverbial conjunctions, which may require commas and/or semi-colons depending on where they are placed within a sentence. Be careful to choose conjunctions that convey the order and emphasis you want within your sentences, paragraphs, and the entire paper.

After you have worked on the style of your writing, you need to concentrate on its correctness. Try to recall typical errors you have seen noted on past papers (You should begin keeping a list of them handy in your writing handbook or journal; a list of common errors may remind you, for instance, if you've had trouble with comma splices in the past). If you know that you continually confuse words that resemble one another or sound alike, study a glossary of usage. These are usually located in writing handbooks. You should also check over your spelling. Don't depend on Spell Check or Grammar Check to find errors for you. With Spell Check, the wrong word may be suggested because your spelling is so far off the mark. With Grammar Check, a sentence may be wrongly labeled fragment. Look carefully for any and all errors, and then work on avoiding them completely. You may want to enlist the help of someone at the Writing Center if you have one at your school.

Publication

After completing your final edits, set is aside for a day or so if that is possible. Read it over again before finally handing your work over for evaluation. When you receive your graded work, study the comments and errors noted on it. See the instructor for anything that needs further clarification, as well as advice on how to improve any errors that have been noted in your paper. Remember that writing is a process; with practice, it becomes easier.

WRITING/CRITICAL THINKING ACTIVITIES

Note: Internet sources are generally transitory, so if a link given for an activity is no longer available, do a search for the source to see if it is elsewhere, or find another suitable source for the activity.

Activity One

In your journal, discuss the writing process as it applies to one of your past papers from this writing class. Be honest as well as specific about each stage and whether your writing process resembled the one discussed in Chapter Three.

Activity Two

1. Read Bob Welch's "Springtree Residents Step Out on Limb," posted on the *Eugene Register Guard* Web site:
   <http://rgweb.registerguard.com/news/2006/07/16/c1.cr.welch.0716.p1.php?section=city egion>
   Discuss the introduction and conclusion strategies Welch uses in this article.

2. Read William Raspberry's "Speaking Two Languages, Both English," posted on the *Washington Post* Web site <http://www.washingtonpost.com/ac2/wp-dyn/A33823-2001Aug19?language=printer>, and discuss the introduction and conclusion strategies he uses in this article.

Activity Three

1. Write an introduction for one of the following thesis statements:

The stimulant Ritalin is an effective treatment for ADD in most children who have been officially diagnosed with ADD.

OR

42

The stimulant Ritalin treats the needs of health professionals, parents, and teachers rather than the needs of children.

2.   Write a conclusion for the thesis statement you chose.

Activity Four

1.   Many strategies exist when writing an introduction, but all are not equally effective for every type of paper. Discuss two strategies that would be more effective for an introduction to an argumentative essay, and be sure to support your choices.

2.   Choose a controversial subject (such as home schooling or the legal drinking age) that you are interested in and do the following:

    o   produce a thesis statement
    o   write an introduction using one of the strategies you recommended in the first question of this activity, and
    o   list three arguments to support your thesis.

REVISION ACTIVITIES

Activity One

The following thesis statements are explanatory or mildly argumentative. Revise them to be strongly argumentative.

1.   Problems exist in our public school system.
2.   It takes money to solve the problems of the homeless.
3.   Some homeless people suffer from mental illness.
4.   Cell phones can be distracting.
5.   Deciding to have an abortion is difficult.
6.   Emergency rooms around the country reported 2,250 injuries associated with motorized scooters.
7.   ADD is a problem in elementary schools.
8.   Computer monitors can be problematic for a user.

43

Activity Two

Read the following introduction and conclusion for an argumentative paper on euthanasia and answer the questions that follow them.

Introduction:

In recent years, euthanasia has triggered a very heated debate. It is a Greek word that means "easy death," but the controversy surrounding it isn't easy at all. Whether the issue is prolonging life mechanically or assisting suicide or active euthanasia, we eventually confront our society's fears toward death itself. Above others, our culture breeds fear and dread of aging and dying. It is not easy for most of the Western world to see death as an inevitable part of life. However, the issues that surround euthanasia are not only about death but are also about one's liberty, right to privacy and control over his or her own body. It is because of these things that one should legally be able to decide to have control over one's own demise.

- o   What is effective about this introductory paragraph?
- o   What strategies could a writer use to make it even more effective?
- o   Give an example of one of these strategies.

Conclusion:

I believe that if in this great country we have the right to life, liberty, and the pursuit of happiness, we have the right to control the conditions of our death as much as we have the right to control the conditions of our living. If procedures similar to the Dutch model can help us avoid unnecessary suffering, it would be worthwhile to work things out with the legal and medical professions. By firmly establishing the right to die in America, an extension of the right to privacy, we are safeguarding such fundamental rights against governmental exploitation. If not a legal law, there is certainly a moral law over one's own body and our life should be subject to our own self-determination. We have a right to end our own life; and if we cannot accomplish the task on our own, at our discretion, another person should have the right to end it for us, as an act of compassion.

- o   What is effective about the concluding paragraph?
- o   What strategies could a writer use to make it even more effective?
- o   Give an example of one of these strategies.

44

STUDENT WEB RESOURCES

Guide to Writing Introductions and Conclusions
<http://depts.gallaudet.edu/Englishworks/writing/introconslu.html>
> Written by Dawn Taylor, English Works! at Gallaudet University provides various strategies to start and end a paper, and examples of each.

Introductions and Conclusions
> Cleveland State University Writing Center provides a thorough discussion of introductions and conclusions at
> > <http://www.csuohio.edu/writingcenter/introcnc.html>
> Roane State Community College OWL provides helpful organization ideas for developing introductions and conclusions at
> > <http://www.rscc.cc.tn.us/owl&writingcenter/OWL/HowtoBegin.html>

Strategies for Writing a Conclusion
<http://leo.stcloudstate.edu/acadwrite/conclude.html>
> LEO, the homepage for The Write Place, the writing center at St. Cloud State University, gives a thorough discussion of conclusion strategies, and examples of each.

Crafting a Thesis
< http://fac.swic.edu/moilessd>
> Steve Moiles of Southwestern Illinois College has designed a Web site containing many useful links on writing, one of which is this site on crafting effective theses statements for argumentative papers.

Adventures in Quoting
<http://fac.swic.edu/moilessd/Qte-prat.html>
> Another link of Steve Moiles' provides a small group exercise devoted to selecting good quotes for research papers.

Writing Vivid Paragraphs
< http://fac.swic.edu/moilessd/secsupp.html>
> Another link of Steve Moiles' provides a guide to developing paragraphs.

45

CHAPTER 7

Locating, Mining, and Citing Sources

This chapter guides students through the process of developing a research question that can lead to a thesis, as discussed in Chapter 6, and provides research resources and an updated guide to handling electronic source material. In higher-level composition courses students will benefit from a walk-through of this chapter, as it will show them what we will be doing throughout the term and how everything leads to the final research paper. This chapter may also be used for its discussion of MLA and APA documentation when the critique and synthesis chapters are covered.

CHAPTER SUMMARY

The Research Process

When writing a research paper, you will use the skills you have already learned, such as summary, analysis, and synthesis. You will go beyond the readings in the text, however, to add breadth and depth to your paper. Depending on your topic, you might use library research, field research (interviews, surveys, etc.), or a combination of the two.

What follows is a list of the steps you will take in planning and writing the paper. Remember that writing is a recursive process; you will not necessarily follow these steps in this order, and you may find yourself backtracking and looping.

Find a Subject. Decide what subject you are going to research and write about. Your text provides you with a wealth of ideas to start with. Use it as a springboard for discovering ideas.

Develop a Research Question. Formulate an important question that you would like to answer through your research. This helps you narrow and focus your topic. The answer to the research question will become your thesis statement.

Conduct Preliminary Research. To help you narrow your topic further and to find out what general information has been written on your topic, look at some general sources on your topic. Consult knowledgeable people, general and specialized encyclopedias, overviews and bibliographies in recent books, the *Bibliographic Index*, and subject heading guides. Consult your reference librarian for suggestions.

47

Conduct Focused Research. Consult books, electronic databases, general and specialized periodicals, biographical indexes, general and specialized dictionaries, government publications, and other appropriate sources. Conduct interviews and surveys, as necessary. In most cases, your research will be based on one or more of the following:

o Books
o Electronic databases (unless you are on campus, you might need a password to access these sources)
o Internet sources (articles and Web sites)
o Articles
o Specialized reference sources
o Interviews and surveys

The sources that you find most useful will probably depend on your topic. Although books will deal with a topic in much greater depth than journal articles will, books take longer to write and publish. If you are doing research on a topic that changes weekly or monthly, you might find that journal articles (whether in paper or electronic form) are more current. On the other hand, you might want the historical background of a subject that only a book can provide. Too many times students use the sources that are the easiest to find, whether they are the best sources or not. While the online encyclopedia Wikipedia is easy to access and can be useful for initial background information, it is not sufficiently reliable nor accurate to use as a source. Rather, you might examine the external links that are often provided at the end of the entry, especially if they are to government or scholarly sites. Let your topic determine what sources work best for your paper.

Develop a Working Thesis. Your question may have changed slightly in the process of conducting initial research—which is natural. As you discover more about your topic, you adjust your perspective. Now that you have done some initial research and are more able to draw conclusions from your research, formulate a working thesis that attempts to respond to your research question.

Develop a Working Bibliography. Keep a working bibliography (either paper or electronic) of your sources. Make this bibliography easy to sort and rearrange. Include all bibliographic information in the bibliography to be used in the "Works Cited" or "References" page.

Evaluate Sources. Attempt to determine the veracity and reliability of your sources (particularly Internet sources). Before taking notes on a source, skim it and check the date of publication. Look for references to other important sources. Use your critical reading skills; check the *Book Review Digest*; look up biographies of authors to check their credentials.

48

Take Notes from Sources. Paraphrase and summarize important information and ideas from your sources. Copy down important quotations. Note page numbers from sources of this quoted and summarized material.

Arrange Your Notes According to Your Outline. Examine your working thesis and write down the components of the thesis that need to be supported in the paper. Determine a writing strategy (comparison/contrast, cause/effect, etc.) for your paper. Develop a working outline of topics to be covered in your paper. Arrange your notes according to this outline.

Write Your Draft. Write the preliminary draft of your paper, working from your notes, according to your outline. Your goal in drafting your paper is to support your thesis by clearly and logically presenting your evidence. Work from your notes, but be sure that the paper uses the sources to present *your* perspective on the topic. Don't worry about perfection at this point. Put your ideas on paper and plan for time to revise extensively.

Avoid Plagiarism. Take care to cite all quoted, paraphrased, and summarized source material, making sure that your own wording and sentence structure differ from those of your sources.

Cite Sources. Use in-text citations and a "Works Cited" or "References" list, according to the conventions of the discipline (or your teacher's instructions).

Revise Your Draft. Use transitional words and phrases to ensure coherence, and check for style. Make sure that the research paper reads smoothly, logically, and clearly from beginning to end, and check for grammatical correctness, punctuation, and spelling.

CHANGES TO MLA

The 3rd edition of the *MLA Style Manual and Guide to Scholarly Publishing*, and the 7th edition of the *MLA Handbook*, include noteworthy changes to citation style:

*The medium of publication, such as "print" and "web," has been added to the works cited entries. In most cases, the insertion of "Web" replaces the need to cite the URL. Indicate URL only when it would be difficult for the reader to access the site without it.

* Italics have replaced underlining in all title elements making MLA consistent with APA guidelines.

*Citation guidelines for articles in online databases obtained through a library subscription have been simplified. Rather than indicate the name of the library and a URL, only the name of the database (italicized) needs to be given, e.g., *JSTOR* and *Project Muse*.

COMPARISON BETWEEN MLA AND APA

Of all professional documentation style manuals, the MLA is the most heavily focused on developing research writing. The APA is less so, focusing on those elements that are specific to psychology; the APA, however, is still aimed at the student writer. Other discipline specific manuals as American Chemical Society and Council of Biological Editors (now Council of Science Editors) assume their audience to primarily be editorial staff, such as editors of journals. Ideally, students should first be familiar with MLA; that is the assumption made by the other discipline styles. Students often feel overwhelmed by the presence of different styles and it is helpful if they understand these differences rhetorically—that styles differ because their audiences and goals differ.

The good news is that there is consistency between MLA and APA. Students can transfer the same rules for use of quotations learned with MLA to APA. APA just adds a "p." to the page number in parentheses: (p. 45). It should be emphasized to students that, yes, a page number is needed for direct quotations; however, using a page number for a paraphrase is optional; this is a major difference between the styles and it may create problems for students. When using APA, students should continue to paraphrase the same way they learned in Chapter 1. Unfortunately, many believe an APA paraphrase requires only minor changes in wording. That fallacy should be addressed. Emphasize that in both MLA and APA students must recast the sentence entirely. Generally, APA prefers that students summarize most source material rather than rely on quotations. The use of large blocks of quoted material by students is a major concern. If block quotes are used, they are formatted as in MLA, except that the left-hand indent is the same as the paragraph indent, one-half inch, not one inch as in MLA.

As with MLA's Works Cited page, there must be a one-to-one correspondence between text references and entries in the Reference page. However, personal communication, such as interviews and letters, are cited only in the text and are not represented on the Reference page. Both styles use similar hanging indentations in the Works Cited and Reference pages. The APA changed over to this format in the 5th edition of the style manual.

The big difference between the two styles is that APA is an author-date system rather than an author-page number system. Currency of sources rather than location in a text is of primary importance, and this is also reflected in the Reference citation entries, which use the same order of citation entry information as MLA, except that the date follows the author's name in parentheses. APA also uses only the initials of authors' first and middle names. There should be a space between each initial.

Commonly, APA documents will cite several authors in a single parenthetical citation. The entries are placed in alphabetical order and separated by a semicolon. Rather than the word "and," APA uses an ampersand (&), but only in the parenthetical citation: (Mack & White, 2001). Notice the comma between the name and the date. If the citation is in the context of the sentence, "and" is used: Mack and White (2001). If there are multiple works by the same author with the same date, the letters a and b are added to the date: (Mack & White, 2001a).

Parenthetical placement of dates follows the name in a sentence: Brown (1999). Citations are placed in each sentence, not at the end of the paragraph. The date need be declared only once per name per paragraph as long as the citation record is transparent. Another pattern is to have the name and date in a parenthesis: (Brown, 1999).

In-text references to book titles and article titles follow standard English capitalization rules. Those titles, however, are lowercased in the Reference page. Only the first letter of a title, a subtitle, and proper nouns are capitalized. Journal titles in both text and References receive standard capitalization of the first letter of all major words.

With the 5th edition of APA and, now with the 7th edition of MLA, there is no underlining. All underlined elements are italicized. Italicize titles of books (not articles), journal titles, volume numbers (but not issue numbers), and the statistical symbols found in the table of statistics.

WRITING/CRITICAL THINKING ACTIVITIES

Note: Internet sources are generally transitory, so if a link given for an activity is no longer available, do a search for the source to see if it is elsewhere or find another suitable source for the activity.

Activity One

1. List three possible arguable research questions for your general topic.

2. List a tentative answer for each of the research questions that you asked in question one. During the research process, you may change your mind about the answer to your research question, but in the final draft of your research paper, this answer will

51

be your thesis statement. This exercise helps you to test the validity or feasibility of your research question.

3. Choose one of your possible research questions and write a proposal for that question. Be sure to answer the following questions (in paragraph form) in your proposal:

4. What is your research question?
   Why did you choose that question to research?
   What do you already know about the topic?
   What do you still need to discover?
   What resources would be most useful as you research your topic? (i.e., name specific medical journals, Web sites, specialists or authorities you might interview, etc.)

Activity Two

Write a proper works cited entry for "Penny Lame" by Dave Simpson <http://www.guardian.co.uk/thebeatles/story/0,11212,1087284,00.htm>.

1. Embed a quotation from "Penny Lame" within a sentence of your own. Be sure to include a proper in-text citation for the article. Include a proper introduction and/or attribution for the quote and an explanatory sentence after the quote.

2. Paraphrase a sentence from "Penny Lame." Be sure to include a proper in-text citation for the article.

3. Summarize "Penny Lame" in one or two sentences and be sure to include a proper in-text citation.

Activity Three

1. Write a proper works cited entry for "Tattoos: Risks and Precautions to Know First" from the Mayo Clinic's Web site: <http://www.mayoclinic.com/health/tattoos-and-piercings/MC00020>.

2. Embed a quotation from "Tattoos: Risks and Precautions to Know First" within a sentence of your own. Be sure to include a proper in-text citation for the article. Include a proper introduction and/or attribution for the quote and an explanatory sentence after the quote.

52

3. Paraphrase a sentence from "Tattoos: Risks and Precautions to Know First." Be sure to include a proper in-text citation for the article.

4. Summarize "Tattoos: Risks and Precautions to Know First" in one or two sentences and be sure to include a proper in-text citation.

REVISION ACTIVITIES

Activity One

Read the following paragraph from a research paper, study the in-text citations as well as the Works Cited entries, and address any errors you find. Discuss any questions you may have about the in-text citations and/or the Works Cited entries:

On March 6, 1996, for the first time in U.S. history, in the case Washington vs. Glucksberg, the U.S. Court of Appeals for the 9th circuit in San Francisco overturned a Washington State law that made assisted suicide a felony. The existing ban on assisted suicide was successfully challenged under the equal protection clause of the Constitution's Fourteenth Amendment. The court noted that, under present law, a dying patient on life support may legally have it removed to facilitate death while another dying patient, not on life support but suffering under equivalent circumstances and equally close to death, has no means by which to end his or her life. The court ruled that bans on assisted suicide constitute a violation of the second patient's equal protection rights under the Fourteenth Amendment (Dority 18). In his majority opinion, appellate Judge Stephen Reinhardt of Los Angeles wrote: "If broad general state policies can be used to deprive a terminally ill individual of the right to make that choice, it is hard to envision where the exercise of arbitrary and intrusive power by the state can be halted" (Weinstein A13). Reinhardt's analysis relies heavily on language drawn from U.S. Supreme Court abortion case, Roe v. Wade, because the issues have "compelling similarities," he wrote. Like the decision of whether or not to have an abortion, the decision how and when to die is one of "the most intimate and personal choices a person may make in a lifetime," a choice "central to personal dignity and autonomy" (Rosen 1).

53

Works Cited

Dority, Barbara. "The Ultimate Civil Liberty." *Humanist* July/August 1997:17-18. Print.

Rosen, Jeffrey. "What Right To Die?" *The New Republic* 24 June 1996. 3 Apr. 2000: 28-31. Web site.

Weinstein, Henry. "Assisted Deaths Ruled Legal: 9th Circuit Lifts Ban on Doctor-Aided Suicide." *Los Angeles Times* 7 Mar. 1996: A1+. Print.

Activity Two

Read the following paragraph from a research paper and study the in-text citations, as well as the Works Cited entries. Go to any online sources given in the Works Cited and check the documentation. Discuss any errors or questions you have about the in-text citations and/or the Works Cited entries:

Did you know that buying such items as toothpaste and cosmetics, you open yourself up to the opportunity to participate in the funding of vivisection? PETA, an international nonprofit organization designed to protect the rights of animals has defined the term as, "the practice of experimenting on live animals" (PETA 1). The American Anti-Vivisection Society reports that between "25 and 50 million animals are killed in American Laboratories each year." Animals such as mice, rabbits, guinea pigs, ferrets, cats, dogs, primates, sheep, cows, and pigs are subjected to the effects of vivisection. Government agencies, corporations, hospitals, the military, and chemical companies conduct the tests. The single largest financier and advocate of vivisection would have to be The National Institutes of Health (NIH). The saddest part about this is that we as taxpayers are paying for the inhumane and cruel treatment of animals. Every time we pay our taxes we are supporting vivisection. The American Anti-Vivisection Society argues that animals are subjected to many painful procedures. Some animals are "burned, starved, irradiated, shocked, mutilated, kept in isolation, poisoned, drugged" and even "electrocuted." The tests range from a monkey's eyes being sewn shut for long periods of times, to a dog's eyes getting burned by radiation, and even go so far as to subject fully conscious cats and dogs to surgery with no anesthetic. When the animals survive, they are used for further testing. Many times, animals such as dogs and cats are silenced through a grotesque procedure, consisting of cutting the animals vocal chords to silence the specimen. The most common type of test used by corporations is the Draize test, named after its inventor, John Draize, who developed the method in 1944. The Draize test is used for testing the safety of products. The test consists

54

of "placing rabbits in stocks that immobilize their heads and then dropping the substance to be tested into one eye, using the other eye as a control" (Regan 199). These tests are often conducted over long periods of time, and the fate of the animal is usually blindness, sometimes death, and always pain. Rabbits are the most commonly used animal involved in Draize testing because their tear ducts are too inefficient to dilute the harmful substances being drained into their eyes.

Works Cited

American Anti-Vivisection Society. 17 Mar. 2000. Web site.

People for the Ethical Treatment of Animals. Web site. N.d

Regan, Tom, and Peter Singer. *Animal Rights and Human Obligations.* New Jersey: Prentice Hall, 1989. Print.

STUDENT WEB RESOURCES

MLA's Frequently Asked Questions about MLA Style
http://www.mla.org/publications/style/style_faq
> The Modern Language Association provides this guide to common questions about using the MLA style. This information has been updated for the 3rd edition of the *MLA Style Manual.*

APA Documentation Style Tips
http://www.apastyle.org/previoustips.html
> The American Psychological Association provides this list of frequently asked questions about using the APA style.

APA Documentation Style Guide to Electronic Sources
http://www.apastyle.org/elecref.html
> The American Psychological Association provides this guide to documenting electronic sources.

APA Citation Format
http://www.lesley.edu/library/guides/citation/apa.html
> Lesley University Library provides APA online handouts for citing sources and for formatting annotated bibliographies.

CHAPTER 8

Practicing Academic Writing: The Changing Landscape of Work in the Twenty-First Century

This chapter provides students with a casebook collection of readings on the topic of the changing American workplace. These articles follow the theme set by "Will Your Job Be Exported?" by Alan Blinder, which is the demonstration article for the summary discussion in Chapter 1 of *A Sequence for Academic Writing*. Experts predict that more and more American jobs will be outsourced to other countries. As students determine their academic majors and prepare for summer jobs and internships, this analysis of employment trends for college-educated job seekers will better prepare them to face globalization in the job market. As our students face an increasingly unsettled employment and economic future, they may be facing tough decisions about their educational future. This chapter's sequence of assignments will take students step-by-step through the development of a source-based argument or analysis. At the same time, by working with the readings and the questions they raise, students will become better informed about changing national trends in employment.

CHAPTER SUMMARY

Synthesis and Analysis Assignments

Students will read a series of explanations and arguments on the topic of "The Changing Landscape of Work in the Twenty-First Century." Then, by responding to a carefully sequenced set of assignments for producing a topic list, summary, paraphrase, critique, and explanatory and argument syntheses, students will prepare to write a source-based argument or analysis on the topic of the changing American workforce. Note that outlines are provided for the culminating assignments in the chapter.

Depending on your student population and type of institution, some students may have a good idea of their majors and future careers, while others will be trying to make decisions about what academic major they should pursue. If your students experience difficulty in narrowing the topic sufficiently, direct them to the short selections provided in this chapter that explores the future changes in the workplace in five different professions. If you have not already had a class discussion on students' college expectations, this may be a good time to revisit Alan S. Blinder's essay in Chapter 1 of *A Sequence of Academic Writing* (a summary of Blinder's essay is presented in this chapter) and discuss the role of college education in the new economy.

57

Additionally, the topic may be "localized," to use the journalistic term, by encouraging students to apply information from "Employment Projections: 2006-2016 Summary" from the Bureau of Labor Statistics (found in Chapter 8 of *A Sequence of Academic Writing*) to their region. Your school's career placement or career planning office can help out with a visit from their office or by providing material on local employment and hiring trends. Students will also benefit from knowing where they can get help with their job and internship searches.

As always, emphasize to students that they should provide documentation in the drafting process. The series of shorter assignments leading up to the longer paper will encourage good referencing habits, but ask students to include source referencing in their paper development. Explain that using sources is an integral part of research paper writing, not an afterthought, and that a failure to document as they write may lead to confusion later when they are writing longer assignments. If they learn these skills now, they will avoid future problems.

WRITING/CRITICAL THINKING ACTIVITIES

Note: Internet sources are generally transitory, so if a link given for an activity is no longer available, do a search for the source to see if it is elsewhere, or find another suitable source for the activity.

Activity One

To encourage students to challenge their own understanding of the readings, the class can be separated into small discussion groups. For the summary assignment, students who are writing about the same article can be grouped together for a rough draft workshop in order to check each other's understanding of the reading. For the critique assignment, the rough draft groups should include students who have adopted different positions on the topic. After working with each other's draft papers, each student should be able to present supporting reasons for and against his or her particular position.

Activity Two

Read Vandana Shiva's essay "The Polarised World of Globalisation: A Response to Friedman's Flat Earth Hypothesis" on the nonprofit *Global Policy Forum* Web site at <http://www.globalpolicy.org/globaliz/define/2005/0510polar.htm>.
What criticisms does Shiva make of Thomas L. Friedman's Flat Earth argument?

58

STUDENT WEB RESOURCES

"Globalization and the Flat World"
<http://www.spu.edu/depts/uc/response/autumn2k7/features/globalization-in-a-flat-world.asp>
> This article by Douglas Downing, professor of Economics was published in the Seattle Pacific University's magazine *Response* in Autumn 2007. Here he considers the role of the educators in preparing students for a changing job market.

"Globalization: 'The World is Flat'"
<http://media.www.jhunewsletter.com/media/storage/paper932/news/2006/03/03/News/Friedman.On.Globalization.the.World.Is.Flat-2242239.shtml>
> In this article, Erica Mitrano reports on a lecture given by Thomas Friedman at the Johns Hopkins University on March 3, 2006.

"Thomas L. Friedman"
<http://topics.nytimes.com/top/opinion/editorialsandoped/oped/columnists/thomaslfriedman/index.html>
> The *New York Times* features a Web site with links to columns written by Friedman for the newspaper.

"Pain from Free Trade Spurs Second Thoughts: Mr. Blinder's Shift Spotlights Warnings of Deeper Downside"
< http://online.wsj.com/article/SB117500805386350446.html >
> This article, by David Wessel and Bob Davis, published March 28, 2007 in the *Wall Street Journal*, suggests some rethinking by Blinder about the effects of globalization.

"Blinder Baloney: Today's Scare Talk of Jobs Outsourcing is Grossly Exaggerated"
<http://findarticles.com/p/articles/mi_m2633/is_4_21/ai_n27440459/pg_1>
> A challenge to Blinder's conclusions by William T. Dickens and Stephen J. Rose, published in *International Economy*, Fall 2007.

59

APPENDIX A: INSTRUCTOR RESOURCES

Web Resources

Provided here are groupings of various Web sites to augment traditional classroom instruction as well as Web-based instruction:

- o **Writing Resources** provides links to all kinds of help for the instructor (and the student) concerning some of the writing required in freshman level composition.
- o **Research Paper Resources** provides links relevant to research based writing— everything from distinguishing scholarly journals from magazines to how to cite electronic resources.
- o **Evaluating Web Resources** provides a variety of helpful sites for instructor and students to determine the usefulness of a Web site.
- o **General Resources** contains a variety of links that don't fit under any of the other groupings.

Writing Resources

Tips for Article Summaries (Valdosta State University)
<http://chiron.valdosta.edu/dtwasieleski/artisumm.htm>
David Wasieleski covers the process of summary writing for psychology students— from picking an article to summarize to revising the summary.

Hunter College Reading/Writing Center
<http://rwc.hunter.cuny.edu/reading-writing/on-line.html>
Hunter College Reading/Writing Center Web site provides many useful handouts on various aspects of writing: the writing process, grammar and mechanics, writing for English courses, the documented essay/research paper, writing across the curriculum, and business and professional writing.

Researched Papers: Integrating Good Sources
<http://jerz.setonhill.edu/writing/academic/sources/integrating.htm>
Professor Dennis G. Jerz of Seton Hill University provides good guidelines for source referencing and examples of how to incorporate quotations. He warns against organizing research papers by source and provides examples with source material coded in color. Additionally, there is a link to a creative hoax Web site to show students how deceptively authoritative a Web site can be.

61

MLA Style: Step-By-Step Instructions
< http://jerz.setonhill.edu/writing/academic/mla_style.html>
>Professor Jerz also provides a very handy guide to how to set up MS-Word to format a paper in MLA style.

Plagiarism (Northwestern University)
<http://www.northwestern.edu/uacc/plagiar.html>
>*Northwestern's "Principles Regarding Academic Integrity" defines plagiarism as "submitting material that in part or whole is not entirely one's own work without attributing those same portions to their correct source." This site provides clear guidelines for proper attribution of sources and plenty of examples.*

Writing to Learn: Encouraging Revision
<www.english.udel.edu/wc/faculty/Newsletters/newsletter2.2.pdf>
>This issue of the *Writing from the Center* newsletter (Feb. 2002) of the University of Delaware Writing Center provides guidelines for revising in the classroom with a student checklist of global revision questions.

Drew University Writing Program Web Resources (Drew University)
<http://www.users.drew.edu/~sjamieso/Webresources.html>
>This Web site contains a great collection of links put together by Sandra Jamieson (many are written by her as well) at Drew University and Rebecca Moore Howard at Syracuse University (with help from Jody Caldwell, Drew Reference Librarian, and Suzanne Updegrove, Drew Academic Technology). Sandra Jamieson stresses that "Any one may use these resources, but bear in mind that they have been adapted for specific courses (English 1-A, English 1, and English 2)" at Drew University. She also supplies links to other sites on the Internet, mostly online writing centers (OWLS) and writing programs.

Research Paper Resources

Columbia University Press
<http://www.columbia.edu/cu/cup/cgos/idx_basic.html>
>Based on *The Columbia Guide to Online Style* by Janice R. Walker and Todd Taylor (Columbia UP, 1998), this site discusses the basics of COS.

Resources for Documenting Sources (Purdue University)
<http://owl.english.purdue.edu/handouts/research/r_docsources.html>
>OWL at Purdue University discusses documentation styles from various disciplines.

Frequently Asked Questions about the MLA Style (Modern Language Association)

<http://www.mla.org/style_faq>

This Modern Language Association Web site provides authoritative answers to commonly asked questions about the MLA documentation style. The site has been recently updated for the newest version of MLA.

Distinguishing Scholarly Journals from Other Periodicals

<http://www.library.cornell.edu/okuref/research/skill20.html>

From the Cornell University Library, this site provides a useful discussion for students on the differences between journals and magazines. Recently, two videos on how to locate and use scholarly and general interest sources have been added.

Media Links

<http://www.users.drew.edu/~sjamieso/medialinks.html>

Another site by Drew University, this one provides a great collection of media links: political commentary sites, magazines and journals from a range of political perspectives, foreign newspapers, wire services, press releases, and online editions of print media.

Recommended Search Engines

<http://www.lib.berkeley.edu/TeachingLib/Guides/Internet/SearchEngines.html>

The University of California at Berkeley provides a tutorial on search engines and how to use them.

Statistics Every Writer Should Know

<http://www.robertniles.com/stats/>

Mathematicians have developed an entire field—statistics—dedicated to getting answers out of numbers. Robert Niles provides a guide to statistics for journalists and other writers.

The Urban Institute

<http://www.urban.org/>

The Institute's Web site contains full-text articles and reports on a variety of social issues.

The Alan Guttmacher Institute
<http://www.guttmacher.org>
> The Alan Guttmacher Institute (AGI) is a nonprofit organization focused on sexual and reproductive health research, policy analysis, and public education. AGI's Web site contains archived articles of *Family Planning Perspectives, International Family Planning Perspectives, The Guttmacher Report on Public Policy* and special reports on sexual and reproductive health and rights.

PBS
<http://www.pbs.org/>
> This site provides the transcripts and informational links for weekly programs aired on *Bill Moyers, Frontline, Washington Week, Science,* and *Nature.*

NPR
<http://www.npr.org>
> This site provides the transcripts and informational links for programs aired on *National Public Radio.*

MSNBC.com
<http://msnbc.com/news/>
> MSNBC.com provides current news reporting from NBC News, MSNBC Cable, CNBC and NBC Sports.

BBC
< http://news.bbc.co.uk>
> For international news from a different perspective, the British Broadcasting Corporation Web site provides reports that often do not get into the U. S. newspapers.

Internet Resources for Writers
<http://www.shortstreet.net/WRsec7.htm>
> This Web site provides general resources for writers on the World Wide Web: directories of sites, libraries, books, periodicals, newspapers, government information, and museums.

Project Vote Smart
<http://www.vote-smart.org/index.htm>
> Project Vote Smart has compiled information on more than 13,000 candidates and elected officials, including the president, members of Congress, governors, and state legislators.

SpeakOut.com
<http://speakout.com/>
> SpeakOut.com, an opinion research company, provides political polls, interactive polls, and articles on a variety of issues (pro and con articles, too).

Writer's Resource Center
<http://www.poewar.com>
> The Writer's Resource Center was created in 1993 to serve the needs of writers on the Internet. It contains thousands of links, along with articles and job opportunities and book reviews dealing with everything from creative writing to technical writing.

The Voice of the Shuttle
<http://vos.ucsb.edu/>
> Since 1994, Alan Liu and members of the English department at University of California-Santa Barbara have been developing the Voice of the Shuttle to provide links to scholarly Web sites in the humanities.

EpistemeLinks.Com
<http://www.epistemelinks.com/Main/MainJour.asp>
> *Devoted to philosophy resources on the Internet, this Web site includes links to over 500 print and electronic journals. You can search by the first initial of each title, or by topic or philosopher area. When searching by topic or philosopher, you can also limit your search to print journals, electronic journals, or both.*

Evaluating Web Resources

Web Evaluation Materials (Wolfgram Memorial Library, Widener University)
<http://www3.widener.edu/Academics/Libraries/Wolfgram_Memorial_Library/Evaluate_Web_Pages/659/>
> This site provides a tutorial on Web site evaluation that shows examples of particular Web sites. It covers the basics of Web evaluation for the different types of Web sites available on the Internet and provides valuable examples of each.

Evaluating Information Found on the Internet
<http://www.library.jhu.edu/researchhelp/general/evaluating/>
> On this Johns Hopkins University Web site, Elizabeth E. Kirk provides guidelines on how to evaluate Web site material. Included in this Web site is "Information and Its

Copyright © 2010, Pearson Education, Inc., Publishing as Longman

Counterfeits," which helps students distinguish real information from its three lookalikes, or counterfeits: propaganda, misinformation, and disinformation.

The ICYouSee Guide to Critical Thinking about What You See on the Web (Ithaca College Library)
<http://www.ithaca.edu/library/training/think.html>

This Web site works well for students as a hands-on activity to learn about Web site evaluation. It is frequently updated by the author, John R. Henderson, Ithaca College Library, with new activities added occasionally.

Urban Legends Reference Pages
<http://www.snopes.com/snopes.asp>

A place to check out Internet rumors and reoccurring bogus claims, not to mention computer virus scares.

Guidelines for Evaluating Web sites
<http://www.iso.gmu.edu/~montecin/webcritique.htm>

Virginia Montecino of George Mason University provides a list of Web sites specializing in Web site evaluation as well as assignments she uses with her students.

General Resources

Dave's ESL Web Guide
<http://www.eslcafe.com/search/>

Dave Sperling provides numerous links to anything related to ESL for teachers and students.

Using Class Email Discussion Lists
<http://www.rc.umd.edu/features/pedagogies/list.html>

The materials on *Romantic Circles* are geared toward courses in Romantic Studies, but they provide useful ideas for teachers in any field to design and use online resources for teaching. In addition, it regularly features different syllabi and Web pages used by Romantics professors (good examples from which to get ideas).

The New Plagiarism
<http://questioning.org/Q4/cov98may.html#anchor161875>

From *The Educational Technology Journal*, this Web page discusses the problem with paper mills and what to do to avoid plagiarism.

66

UWC Handouts on Writing and Grammar (University Writing Center at Central Florida)

<http://www.uwc.ucf.edu/Writing%20Resources/handout_home.htm>
> *UWC consultants have prepared a series of useful handouts on all aspects of writing.*

College Composition and Communication (CCC)

< http://www.ncte.org/college>
> Online Web site for composition's professional organization. Contains book reviews.

Kairos: A Journal of Rhetoric, Technology, and Pedagogy

< http://kairos.technorhetoric.net>
> A referred online journal that explores the intersections of rhetoric, technology, and teaching.

WAC Clearinghouse

<http://wac.colostate.edu/>
> The WAC Clearinghouse brings together five journals, four book series, and resources for teachers who use writing in their courses.

Silva Rhetoricae: The Forest of Rhetoric

<http://humanities.byu.edu/rhetoric/silva.htm>
This online rhetoric, provided by Dr. Gideon Burton of Brigham Young University, is a guide to the terms of classical and renaissance rhetoric.

APPENDIX B: INSTRUCTOR RESOURCES
Assignment Ideas and Sample Syllabi

Issue Proposal Assignment

Before beginning the issue proposal, formulate a research question. Your issue must be current (within the last 5 years). **You must have my approval** before beginning your Issue Proposal. The question you choose will be the focus of your research paper, so take some time to consider your research question.

An issue proposal consists of three parts:

1. The first paragraph introduces the issue you will be handling in your research paper. It should be written in third person. You need to discuss some of the history of this issue (for example, you will need to discuss some recent school shootings if you are dealing with gun control). You will need to end this discussion with your research question.

2. The second paragraph explains why this issue is compelling to you. You need to write this in first person. Why did you pick this issue? Do you have some experience in it either personally or vicariously? Is it related somehow to the field you are entering? Remember that it is important to have an interest in your issue. (You will be working with it for many weeks.)

3. The third paragraph explains your research plan: what **you think** you need to learn to answer your research question and how do you plan to get that information. This needs to be written in first person. Consider the sources you might have to consult: journals (name some), newspapers (name some), Internet (name some Web sites), authorities in the field, television programs, etc.

Annotated List of Works Cited Assignment

An Annotated List of Works Cited for your research paper must include **ten possible sources**. Your sources must be current (no older than 2000) articles from general and specialized periodicals (see *SAW*, Chapter 7 for definitions of these), either hard copy or online versions. You may also use articles, links, or even an entire Web site from the Internet, but make sure you do a thorough evaluation of the Web site before choosing it or any articles/links from it. You are not committing yourself to using these sources in your research paper, just indicating that they appear to be relevant to your research paper. As I indicated above, your sources must be dated 2000 or later, but with my permission,

68

you may use earlier sources. To format your Annotated List of Works Cited, begin with a paragraph indicating the parameters of your research: what you will cover and what you will not cover. Then set up the bibliographic citation for each source following MLA guidelines, placing the sources in alphabetical order. After each source, provide an annotation, a short paragraph (3 or 4 typed lines), for each article/link/Web site that explains why this source is potentially useful for *your* research paper. The annotation will not be a comprehensive summary; rather it will assess how useful the source is for your particular research project.

Critique Assignment

See the "**Writing Assignment: Critique**" in Chapter 2 of *A Sequence for Academic Writing*. Follow the instructions given to write your critique. Review the discussion of critique writing and examine the sample critique. Critique Ryan's editorial using some of the Web addresses given below for evidence to support your critique. In addition, you may also use personal experience for evidence to support your critique. You will need to cite your sources using MLA in-text documentation and a Works Cited page.

Arnold, Gina. "Dance of the Sugar Plum Anorexics: A Mother Sues the San Francisco Ballet School to Demand Diversity of Body Type." 21 July 2006. 14 Dec. 2000. <http://archive.salon.com/mwt/feature/2000/12/14/ballet_body/index.html>.

Bentley, Toni. "Counterpunch: Critic's Argument for Heftier Dancers is Thin." *Los Angeles Times* 16 April 2001. <http://www.tonibentley.com/pages/journalism_pages/journalism_latimes.html>.

Epstein, Edward. "Girl Fights For a Chance to Dance: Complaint Filed Over School's Body-Type Rules." *San Francisco Chronicle* 7 December 2000. A1. 21 July 2006 <http://www.sfgate.com/cgi-bin/article.cgi?file=/chronicle/archive/2000/12/07/MNW134594.DTL>.

Felciano, Rita. "School for Sylphs?—San Francisco Ballet School Discrimination Case." *Dance Magazine* April 2001. 21 July 2006 <http://findarticles.com/p/articles/mi_m1083/is_4_75/ai_72273983>.

San Francisco Ballet. "Ballet School." Web site. <http://www.sfballet.org/balletschool/school/history.asp>.

Speer, Dean and Francis Timlin. "Gloria Govrin, Associate Director, San Francisco Ballet School: Govrin's Glorious Students: A Pedagogue's View." *Ballet Dance Magazine* May 2005. 21 July 2006. <http://www.ballet-dance.com/200505/articles/GloriaGovrin20041200.htm>.

Synthesis Assignment

Read Chapter 8 Practicing Academic Writing of *A Sequence for Academic Writing*. Using the changing landscape of work in the twenty-first century articles from Chapter 8 of *A Sequence for Academic Writing*, write an argument synthesis using the Guidelines for Writing Syntheses found in chapter 3. After reading at least four articles (you may need to read more than four if no thesis comes to mind that involves ideas of at least three of the articles), formulate an argumentative thesis making use of one of the four options given in the argument synthesis assignment in Chapter 8. (You must clearly state which position you are taking.) E-mail me if you aren't sure your thesis is clear. You must support your thesis with material from at least three of the articles from Chapter 8 of *A Sequence for Academic Writing* and/or the other Web links. In addition, you may also use personal experience for evidence to support your synthesis (this would not be considered one of the three required sources). You will need to cite your sources, using MLA in-text documentation and a works cited page.

Oral Presentation Assignment

For this assignment, you will present the thesis and the most important arguments from your research paper orally. Avoid reading from your essay and make eye contact with your audience. You may use note cards; I don't want you to bring in a copy of your research paper from which to read. Too much reading will automatically drop your presentation grade a letter grade. You will be expected to speak for 5 to 7 minutes. Points may be deducted for reports being either too short or too long. Practice to make your report fit the time requirements. Dress appropriately for an oral presentation.

Sample Syllabi

Sample Web-Based and Traditional Syllabi for a Semester Course

Composition II/Web-Based Sample Syllabus

Note: This is not a complete entire syllabus. Included here are the minor assignments, major assignments, reading assignments, procedures and policies, etc. that are relevant to a Web-based Composition II course. All references to "Click here ..." pertain to assignments, sample papers, handouts, and online sources that students would access from the Internet. When the syllabus is posted online, all discussions of assignments are highlighted in red, all of the due dates are blue, and all of the sample assignments and handouts are pink.

Course: xxx	Instructor: xxx
Course Number: xxx	Credits: x
Prerequisite: xxx	Office: xxx
Office Phone: xxx-xxxx	Office Hours: xxx

Abbreviations in Syllabus

SAW = *A Sequence for Academic Writing*
DB1 = Discussion Board One
DB2 = Discussion Board Two

Evaluation

Written work will provide the major basis for the course grade. The highest possible points for each assignment follow.
 Note: All assignments must be single-spaced, typed (using a computer and a standard 12 pt. font), and emailed.

Attendance (participation on DB1 14 weeks @ 12.5 pts. each week) 175 pts
Homework Assignments (accessed through the CW; best 10 out of 12 @ 10 pts. a piece) 100 pts

Major assignments:

Issue Proposal (500 to 600 words; must follow assigned format) 50 pts
Annotated List of Works Cited (10 entries; must follow assigned format) 100 pts

71

Critique (500 to 750 words; must follow assigned format) 125 pts
Synthesis (750 to 1000) words) 125 pts
Researched Argument Paper (2000 to 2500 words) 225 pts
Oral Presentation (5 to 7 minutes) 100 pts
Total points   1000

Final Grading Scale
1000-900 = A 899-800 = B 799-700 = C 699-600 = D 599-0 = F

Course Procedures and Policies
For attendance in this class, you earn points each week by participating on DB1 no earlier than Sunday but no later than Thursday at midnight. After Thursday, I post responses/answers to DB1, so no further points can be earned. You must respond to DB1 assignments listed each week in the syllabus, and you must respond to at least two other students' responses (except where noted). All assignments are due when noted on the syllabus; you have until midnight to e-mail me your assignment. Late assignments will be accepted, but 10% will be subtracted for every day an assignment is late. (This does not include DB1 assignments.) I expect you to communicate with me by e-mail, DB2, or in person during my office hours for any questions you may have concerning assignments.

Instructional Methods

Students will read, prepare for, and complete assignments in a timely fashion, submitting the results of their work by e-mail, depending on assignment requirements. Each assignment will be returned to the student by e-mail within one week of its due date. (If you turn an assignment in earlier, it may be graded earlier if I have time.) The graded research papers will be not be e-mailed. (It is too hard to grade lengthy papers online.) I will keep them until the end of the following semester for you to pick up at my office. You and I must recognize the possibility of "computer problems" and find a reasonable way to work around them. **Always** keep a copy of any assignment you e-mailed (use "copy" or "sent" e-mail folders), so if I don't receive an assignment of yours, you have proof that you attempted to send it to avoid losing points for lateness. Always print a copy as a backup in case an assignment doesn't get to me. Also, keep all e-mail I send you, graded assignments or whatever, for your own protection. My computer has been known to have a meltdown or two. You also need to have a backup plan in case your computer has problems.

For emergencies, locate a campus computer lab. Keep its hours and days handy.

72

Week One

Go to DB1 and write a short introduction about yourself for the other students and me. Carefully consider your audience and what impression you want to give. Check DB1 periodically throughout the week, read some of the introductions, and then respond to at least one other student's introduction. (For example, maybe you have something in common with another student.) Use your first and last name and always give your e-mail address when using the discussion boards, so we all know who you are.

Note: You may want to work on your responses in Word, so you can spell check them and carefully proofread before you post them to the DB1. Always use complete sentences and a clear subject line.

Week Two

For your first homework assignment, go to Chapter 7: Locating, Mining, and Citing Sources, follow the instructions in Exercise 7.1, and write a research question for each of the topics listed. Think of controversial questions when doing this assignment. Proofread your answers and when you are ready, e-mail your homework to me. Enter all e-mail addresses carefully, and always e-mail a copy of your results to yourself. Short answers are all that is expected, but I want complete sentences throughout. This is considered a minor assignment (worth 10 points) that will help you prepare for your issue proposal assignment. **Note**: You may want to compose your answers in Word, so you can spell check them and carefully proofread before you paste them in the e-mail text boxes. Post any questions about possible research topics you are considering on DB1. Remember to comment or make suggestions concerning the postings of at least two other students.

Week Three

Homework #1 due. Writing an Issue Proposal (Click here for Issue Proposal Assignment). Click here for a good example of an issue proposal from a previous semester. Read SAW Chapter 5. If your proposal was based on an arguable research question you want to pursue AND I approved it, you can use it as a rough draft of your issue proposal. Click on the two sample proposals: Sample A & Sample B. Make one posting with comments about both sample proposals on DB1. As possible questions, consider the following: Does each proposal cover the items I outlined in the issue proposal assignment? If they do, is there enough? Is there too much? If they don't, what is missing? Support your answers. Use DB2 for any other questions you might have about your issue proposal or anything else related to this course.

Week Four

Read SAW Chapter 1. For your second homework assignment, go to Exercise 1.1 and write a summary of the passage. On DB1 this week, respond to the following question: Can a writer be objective when summarizing? Support your answer. I will be reading

73

many summaries (those written by you students) of the same article. Some of your summaries will be longer, some shorter, some with more detail, some with less, etc. How do you account for these differences? Support your answer.

Week Five
Homework #2 due. Issue Proposal due. Evaluating electronic sources. Check out the following two sites for help with evaluating Web sources: *Evaluating Information Found on the Internet* & *The ICYouSee Guide to Critical Thinking about What You See on the Web*. For your third homework assignment, go to Chapter 7, Exercise 7.3 and follow the instructions. For your fourth homework assignment, go to Chapter 7, Exercise 7.4, and then evaluate Web pages according to the criteria list. On DB1 this week, make one posting that includes a short evaluation about each Web site you analyzed for homework #4. Comment on the evaluations of two other students once you have posted your own.

Week Six
Homework #3 and #4 due. Compiling an Annotated List of Works Cited. For your fifth homework assignment, go to Chapter 1: Summary, Paraphrase, and Quotation, Exercise 1.6 and paraphrase three passages. Discuss your experiences to Homework #5 on DB1. Comment on the postings of two other students once you have posted your own.

Week Seven
Homework #5 due. Taking notes. Documenting MLA Style and APA Style. Before you attempt homework # 6, see Chapter 7 of SAW for an example of how to format an MLA works cited entry for an article from an online magazine and how to format an APA reference entry. For your sixth homework assignment, select 4 annotated bibliography entries and format them for both MLA and APA . No DB1 activity for this week.

Week Eight
Homework #6 due. Using sources. Read SAW on how to paraphrase in Chapter 1. Documenting in-text MLA Style. Critiquing an argument. Read Chapter 2 in SAW. Writing a Critique (Click here for Critique Assignment). For your seventh homework assignment, go to Chapter 2: Critical Reading and Critique, Exercise 2.5 and respond. Question #6 involves writing a critique, which should be multi-paragraphed. On DB1 this week, answer the following two questions in one posting: Can you disagree with an author's view and still evaluate the presentation of his argument fairly? How would you go about writing such a critique?

Week Nine
Annotated List of Works Cited due. Homework #7 due. For your eighth homework assignment, go to Chapter 2: Critical Reading and Critique, and critique Beres' essay. On DB1, comment on whether the model critique contains the elements of argument

74

discussed in the SAW. Does the sample paper follow the format discussed? Be prepared to support your answer and comment on two of the other students' comments as well.

Week Ten
Critique due. Homework #8 due. Writing a Researched Argument Paper (Click here for Research Paper Assignment). Click on the following paper for a good example of a research paper: Animal Rights. Read Chapter 6 of SAW on Writing as a Process and Chapter 8: Practicing Academic Writing. For your ninth homework assignment, go to Chapter 6, Exercise 6.5 and 6.6, follow instructions and write an introduction and a conclusion. On DB1, discuss what techniques you might use in your research paper to start your paper and end your paper. Comment on at least two other students' ideas as well.

Week Eleven
Homework #9 due. Writing an Argument Synthesis (click here for Synthesis Assignment. Read Chapter 4 of SAW. Read the following handout: Pathos, Logos, and Ethos. For your tenth homework assignment, go to Chapter 6: Writing as a Process, click on "Writing/Critical Thinking Activities," click on "Activity 3," and then answer the question in the text box provided. Look at the following example of an argument and on DB1 discuss any examples of pathos, logos, and ethos you see.

Week Twelve
Homework #10 due. Continue to work on research paper. For your eleventh homework assignment, go to Chapter 4: Argument Synthesis, Exercise 4.1 and follow directions. On DB1, in one posting, give us your thesis (label it so we know it is your thesis), one of your argument paragraphs, and one of your counterargument with refutation paragraphs for peer review. Comment on at least two other students' arguments and counters with refutation. I will comment on it and send it back to you ASAP.

Week Thirteen
Homework #11 due. Rough draft of research paper due. Work on Oral Presentation (click here for Oral Presentation Assignment), which may be given via in person or videotaped (to be mailed or dropped off). Click on oral presentations and speech anxiety for helpful tips. For your twelfth homework assignment, go to Chapter 4: Argument Synthesis and do Exercises 4.2 and 4.3.

Week Fourteen
Synthesis due. Homework #12 due. Work on research paper. Read over the following articles and examine the MLA documentation, both in-text and the works cited: Article A

& Article B. On DB1, discuss any errors you notice or questions you have concerning their MLA documentation. Comment on at least two other students' postings as well.

Week Fifteen

Research Paper due. Work on and practice your oral presentation. Post an outline of your entire oral presentation to DB1 for feedback from other students. Critique at least one other student's outline.

Week Sixteen

Oral Presentation due via in person or videotaped (to be mailed or dropped off). For your last assignment on the DB1, you only need to post once. No responses to other students are necessary. On DB1, if you had had more time to work on your research paper, what changes would you have made?

Composition II/ Traditional Syllabus

Abbreviations in Syllabus
SAW = *A Sequence for Academic Writing*

Evaluation
Written work will provide the major basis for the course grade. The highest possible points for each assignment follow. **Please note**: All assignments must be single-spaced, typed (using a computer and a standard 10 or 12 pt. font), and e-mailed.

In-Class Writing assignments (accessed through the CW; 20 @ 10 pts. a piece) 200
Issue Proposal (500 to 600 words; must follow assigned format) 100
Annotated List of Works Cited (10 entries; must follow assigned format) 100
Critique (500 to 750 words; must follow assigned format) 125
Synthesis (750 to 1000) words) 150
Researched Argument Paper (2000 to 2500 words) 225
Oral Presentation (7 to 10 minutes) 125
Total points 1000

Final Grading Scale
1000-900 = A 899-800 = B 799-700 = C 699-600 = D 599-0 = F

Week One
Discuss purpose of this class. Do research for possible papers topics for Argumentative Research Paper. Brainstorm controversial subjects for research paper

Week Two
For your first homework assignment, go to Chapter 7: Locating, Mining, and Citing Sources, follow the instructions in Exercise 7.1, and write a research question for each of the topics listed. Think of controversial questions when doing this assignment. Proofread your answers before handing your assignment in.

Week Three
Read Chapter 7 of *SAW*. Discuss research paper process. Discuss the strengths and weaknesses of two sample proposals: Sample A & Sample B.

Week Four
Read *SAW* Chapter 1. For your second homework assignment, go to Exercise 1.1 and write a summary of the passage. In class, respond to the following questions. Can a writer be objective when summarizing? Support your answer. I will be reading many summaries

(those written by you students) of the same article. Some of your summaries will be longer, some shorter, some with more detail, some with less, etc. How do you account for these differences? Support your answer.

Week Five
Homework #2 due. Issue Proposal due. Evaluating electronic sources. Check out the following two sites for help with evaluating Web sources: *Evaluating Information Found on the Internet* & *The ICYouSee Guide to Critical Thinking About What You See on the Web*. For your third homework assignment, go to Chapter 7, Exercise 7.3 and follow the instructions. For your fourth homework assignment, go to Chapter 7, Exercise 7.4, and then evaluate Web pages according to the criteria list. In class, bring one evaluation about each Web site you analyzed for homework #4. Comment on the evaluations of two other students in groups.

Week Six
Homework #3 and #4 due. Compiling an Annotated List of Works Cited. For your fifth homework assignment, go to Chapter 1: Summary, Paraphrase, and Quotation, Exercise 1.6 and paraphrase three passages. Discuss your experiences to Homework #5 in class and comment on the postings of two other students in groups.

Week Seven
Homework #5 due. Taking notes. Documenting MLA Style and APA Style. Before you attempt homework # 6, see Chapter 7 of SAW for an example of how to format an MLA works cited entry for an article from an online magazine and how to format an APA reference entry. For your sixth homework assignment, select 4 annotated bibliography entries and format them for both MLA and APA.

Week Eight
Homework #6 due. Using sources. Read SAW on how to paraphrase in Chapter 1. Documenting in-text MLA Style. Critiquing an argument. Read Chapter 2 in SAW. Writing a Critique. For your seventh homework assignment, go to Chapter 2: Critical Reading and Critique, Exercise 2.5 and respond. Question #6 involves writing a critique, which should be multi-paragraphed. In class this week, answer the following two questions in one posting: Can you disagree with an author's view and still evaluate the presentation of his argument fairly? How would you go about writing such a critique?

Week Nine

Annotated List of Works Cited due. Homework #7 due. For your eighth homework assignment, go to Chapter 2: Critical Reading and Critique, and critique Beres' essay. In class, comment on whether the model critique contains the elements of argument discussed in the SAW. Does the sample paper follow the format discussed? Be prepared to support your answer and comment on two of the other students' comments as well.

Week Ten

Critique due. Homework #8 due. Writing a Researched Argument Paper. See example research paper. Read Chapter 6 of SAW on Writing as a Process and Chapter 8: Practicing Academic Writing. For your ninth homework assignment, go to Chapter 6, Exercise 6.5 and 6.6, follow instructions and write an introduction and a conclusion. In class, discuss what techniques you might use in your research paper to start your paper and end your paper. Comment on at least two other students' ideas as well.

Week Eleven

Homework #9 due. Writing an Argument Synthesis. Read Chapter 4 of SAW. Read the handout on Pathos, Logos, and Ethos. For your tenth homework assignment, go to Chapter 6:Writing as a Process," click on "Writing/Critical Thinking Activities," click on "Activity 3," and then answer the question in the text box provided. Look at the following example of an argument and, in class, discuss any examples of pathos, logos, and ethos you see.

Week Twelve

Homework #10 due. Continue to work on research paper. For your eleventh homework assignment, go to Chapter 4: Argument Synthesis, Exercise 4.1 and follow directions. Then hand in your thesis (label it so we know it is your thesis), one of your argument paragraphs, and one of your counterargument with refutation paragraphs for peer review. Comment on at least two other students' arguments and counters with refutation. I will comment on it and send it back to you ASAP.

Week Thirteen

Homework #11 due. Rough draft of research paper due. Work on Oral Presentation, which may be given in person or videotaped (to be mailed or dropped off). Click on oral presentations and speech anxiety for helpful tips. For your twelfth homework assignment, go to Chapter 4: Argument Synthesis and do Exercises 4.2 and 4.3.

Week Fourteen
Synthesis due..Homework #12 due. Work on research paper. Read over the following articles and examine the MLA documentation, both in-text and the works cited: Article A & Article B. In class, discuss any errors you notice or questions you have concerning their MLA documentation.

Week Fifteen
Research Paper due. Work on outlines for oral presentations, and practice your oral presentation in class.

Week Sixteen
Oral Presentation due.